MW01703510

Presented

to

by

Date

Occasion

Table Of Contents

YOUR CHILDREN

Unless otherwise indicated, all Scripture quotations are taken from the King James Version of the Bible.
The Father's Topical Bible · ISBN 1-56394-165-1/B-35
Copyright © 1999 by *MIKE MURDOCK*
All publishing rights belong exclusively to Wisdom International
Published by The Wisdom Center · P.O. Box 99 • Denton, Texas 76202
1-888-WISDOM 1 (1-888-947-3661) · Website: thewisdomcenter.tv

Printed in the United States of America.
All rights reserved under International Copyright Law. Contents and/or cover may not be reproduced in whole or in any part in any form without the express written consent of the Publisher.
0403◊10k

YOUR RELATIONSHIP TO GOD

1

YOUR PRAYER LIFE

Now Hannah, she spake in her heart; only her lips moved, but her voice was not heard: therefore Eli thought she had been drunken. *1 Samuel 1:13*

Seek the Lord and His strength, seek His face continually.
1 Chronicles 16:11

If My people, which are called by My name, shall humble themselves, and pray, and seek My face, and turn from their wicked ways; then will I hear from heaven, and will forgive their sin, and will heal their land.

2 Chronicles 7:14

When Thou saidst, Seek ye My face; my heart said unto Thee, Thy face, Lord, will I seek. *Psalm 27:8*

Yet the Lord will command His lovingkindness in the daytime, and in the night His song shall be with me, and my prayer unto the God of my life.

Psalm 42:8

But thou, when thou prayest, enter into thy closet, and when thou hast shut thy door, pray to thy Father which is in secret; and thy Father which seeth in secret shall reward thee openly.

Matthew 6:6

And He spake a parable unto them to this end, that men ought always to pray, and not to faint; *Luke 18:1*

And Mary said, My soul doth

magnify the Lord,

And my spirit hath rejoiced in God my Saviour. *Luke 1:46,47*

Likewise the Spirit also helpeth our infirmities: for we know not what we should pray for as we ought: but the Spirit itself maketh intercession for us with groanings which cannot be uttered. *Romans 8:26*

Praying always with all prayer and supplication in the Spirit, and watching thereunto with all perseverance and supplication for all saints;

Ephesians 6:18

Be careful for nothing; but in every thing by prayer and supplication with thanksgiving let your requests be made known unto God. *Philippians 4:6*

Continue in prayer, and watch in the same with thanksgiving;

Colossians 4:2

Pray without ceasing.

1 Thessalonians 5:17

I will therefore that men pray every where, lifting up holy hands, without wrath and doubting.

1 Timothy 2:8

Let us therefore come boldly unto the throne of grace, that we may obtain mercy, and find grace to help in time of need. *Hebrews 4:16*

But ye, beloved, building up yourselves on your most holy faith, praying in the Holy Ghost, *Jude 1:20*

2

YOUR STUDY OF GOD'S WORD

And Moses came and told the people all the words of the Lord, and all the judgments: and all the people answered with one voice, and said, All the words which the Lord hath said will we do. *Exodus 24:3*

Ye shall not add unto the word which I command you, neither shall ye diminish ought from it, that ye may keep the commandments of the Lord your God which I command you.
Deuteronomy 4:2

And these words, which I command thee this day, shall be in thine heart:

And He humbled thee, and suffered thee to hunger, and fed thee with manna, which thou knewest not, neither did thy fathers know; that He might make thee know that man doth not live by bread only, but by every word that proceedeth out of the mouth of the Lord doth man live.

Deuteronomy 8:3

The secret things belong unto the Lord our God: but those things which are revealed belong unto us and to our children for ever, that we may do all the words of this law. *Deuteronomy 29:29*

But the word is very nigh unto thee, in thy mouth, and in thy heart, that thou mayest do it.

Deuteronomy 30:14

This book of the law shall not depart out of thy mouth; but thou shalt meditate therein day and night, that thou mayest observe to do according to all that is written therein: for then thou shalt make thy way prosperous,

and then thou shalt have good success.
Joshua 1:8

Be ye mindful always of His covenant; the word which He commanded to a thousand generations;
1 Chronicles 16:15

Receive, I pray thee, the law from His mouth, and lay up His words in thine heart. *Job 22:22*

Therefore whosoever heareth these sayings of Mine, and doeth them, I will liken him unto a wise man, which built his house upon a rock:
Matthew 7:24

Heaven and earth shall pass away: but My words shall not pass away.
Mark 13:31

So then faith cometh by hearing, and hearing by the word of God.
Romans 10:17

3

Your Attitude Toward Praise And Worship

Give unto the Lord the glory due unto His name: bring an offering, and come before Him: worship the Lord in the beauty of holiness.

1 Chronicles 16:29

It came even to pass, as the trumpeters and singers were as one, to make one sound to be heard in praising and thanking the Lord; and when they lifted up their voice with the trumpets and cymbals and instruments of musick, and praised the Lord, saying, For He is good; for His mercy endureth for ever: that then the house was filled with a cloud, even the house of the Lord;

2 Chronicles 5:13

O come, let us worship and bow down: let us kneel before the Lord our maker. *Psalm 95:6*

Enter into His gates with thanksgiving, and into His courts with praise: be thankful unto Him, and bless His name. *Psalm 100:4*

Oh that men would praise the Lord for His goodness, and for His wonderful works to the children of men!

Psalm 107:8

I will worship toward Thy holy temple, and praise Thy name for Thy lovingkindness and for Thy truth: for Thou hast magnified Thy word above all Thy name. *Psalm 138:2*

Praise ye the Lord. Praise God in His sanctuary: praise Him in the firmament of His power.

Praise Him for His mighty acts: praise Him according to His excellent greatness.

Praise Him with the sound of the trumpet: praise Him with the psaltery and harp.

Praise Him with the timbrel and dance: praise Him with stringed instruments and organs.

Praise Him upon the loud cymbals: praise Him upon the high sounding cymbals.

Let every thing that hath breath praise the Lord. Praise ye the Lord.

Psalm 150:1-6

And Jesus answered and said unto him, Get thee behind me, satan: for it is written, Thou shalt worship the Lord thy God, and Him only shalt thou serve.

Luke 4:8

But the hour cometh, and now is, when the true worshippers shall worship the Father in Spirit and in truth: for the Father seeketh such to worship Him.

God is a Spirit: and they that worship Him must worship Him in Spirit and in truth. *John 4:23,24*

What is it then? I will pray with the Spirit, and I will pray with the understanding also: I will sing with the Spirit, and I will sing with the understanding also. *1 Corinthians14:15*

For we are the circumcision, which worship God in the Spirit, and rejoice in Christ Jesus, and have no confidence in the flesh. *Philippians 3:3*

I will therefore that men pray every where, lifting up holy hands, without wrath and doubting.
1 Timothy 2:8

Ye also, as lively stones, are built up a spiritual house, an holy priesthood, to offer up spiritual sacrifices, acceptable to God by Jesus Christ. *1 Peter 2:5*

4

YOUR HOURLY OBEDIENCE TO GOD

Now therefore, if ye will obey My voice indeed, and keep My covenant, then ye shall be a peculiar treasure unto Me above all people: for all the earth is Mine: *Exodus 19:5*

Thou hast commanded us to keep Thy precepts diligently. *Psalm 119:4*

He that keepeth the commandment keepeth his own soul; but he that despiseth His ways shall die. *Proverbs 19:16*

If ye be willing and obedient, ye shall eat the good of the land:
Isaiah 1:19

Whosoever therefore shall break one of these least commandments, and shall teach men so, he shall be called the least in the kingdom of heaven: but whosoever shall do and teach them, the same shall be called great in the kingdom of heaven. *Matthew 5:19*

For whosoever shall do the will of My Father which is in heaven, the same is My brother, and sister, and mother.
Matthew 12:50

If ye love Me, keep My commandments.

Jesus answered and said unto him, If a man love Me, he will keep My words: and My Father will love him, and We will come unto him, and make Our abode with him. *John 14:15,23*

If ye keep My commandments, ye shall abide in My love; even as I have kept My Father's commandments, and abide in His love.

Ye are My friends, if ye do

whatsoever I command you. *John 15:10,14*

Then Peter and the other apostles answered and said, We ought to obey God rather than men. *Acts 5:29*

And whatsoever we ask, we receive of Him, because we keep His commandments, and do those things that are pleasing in His sight. *1 John 3:22*

5

WHEN YOU NEED ASSURANCE OF ETERNAL LIFE

For as the lightning cometh out of the east, and shineth even unto the west; so shall also the coming of the Son of man be. *Matthew 24:27*

And beginning at Moses and all the prophets, He expounded unto them in all the scriptures the things concerning Himself. *Luke 24:27*

And he that reapeth receiveth wages, and gathereth fruit unto life eternal: that both he that soweth and he that reapeth may rejoice together. *John 4:36*

Then they willingly received Him into the ship: and immediately the ship was at the land whither they went.

John 6:21

And I give unto them eternal life; and they shall never perish, neither shall any man pluck them out of My hand. *John 10:28*

And if I go and prepare a place for you, I will come again, and receive you unto Myself; that where I am, there ye may be also. *John 14:3*

And this is life eternal, that they might know Thee the only true God, and Jesus Christ, Whom Thou hast sent. *John 17:3*

For yet a little while, and He that shall come will come, and will not tarry.

Hebrews 10:37

Be ye also patient; stablish your hearts: for the coming of the Lord draweth nigh. *James 5:8*

And when the chief Shepherd shall appear, ye shall receive a crown of glory that fadeth not away. *1 Peter 5:4*

But the day of the Lord will come as a thief in the night; in the which the heavens shall pass away with a great noise, and the elements shall melt with fervent heat, the earth also and the works that are therein shall be burned up. *2 Peter 3:10*

Beloved, now are we the sons of God, and it doth not yet appear what we shall be: but we know that, when He shall appear, we shall be like Him; for we shall see Him as He is. *1 John 3:2*

YOUR QUALITIES

6

LOVING

He hath said in his heart, God hath forgotten: He hideth His face; He will never see it. *Psalm 10:11*

Blessed is he that considereth the poor: the Lord will deliver him in time of trouble. *Psalm 41:1*

Better is a dinner of herbs where love is, than a stalled ox and hatred therewith. *Proverbs 15:17*

Withhold not good from them to whom it is due, when it is in the power of thine hand to do it.

Say not unto thy neighbour, Go, and come again, and to morrow I will give; when thou hast it by thee.

Proverbs 3:27,28

Brethren, if a man be overtaken in a fault, ye which are spiritual, restore such an one in the spirit of meekness; considering thyself, lest thou also be tempted.

Bear ye one another's burdens, and so fulfil the law of Christ.

As we have therefore opportunity, let us do good unto all men, especially unto them who are of the household of faith. *Galatians 6:1,2,10*

And walk in love, as Christ also hath loved us, and hath given Himself for us an offering and a sacrifice to God for a sweet-smelling savour.

Ephesians 5:2

And the Lord make you to increase and abound in love one toward another, and toward all men, even as we do toward you: *1 Thessalonians 3:12*

But as touching brotherly love ye need not that I write unto you: for ye yourselves are taught of God to love one another. *1 Thessalonians 4:9*

But whoso hath this world's good, and seeth his brother have need, and shutteth up his bowels of compassion from him, how dwelleth the love of God in him?

My little children, let us not love in word, neither in tongue; but in deed and in truth. *1 John 3:17,18*

Beloved, let us love one another: for love is of God; and every one that loveth is born of God, and knoweth God.

He that loveth not knoweth not God; for God is love. *1 John 4:7,8*

7

UNDERSTANDING

Be ye not as the horse, or as the mule, which have no understanding: whose mouth must be held in with bit and bridle, lest they come near unto thee.
Psalm 32:9

Through Thy precepts I get understanding: therefore I hate every false way.
Psalm 119:104

Happy is the man that findeth wisdom, and the man that getteth understanding.

She is a tree of life to them that lay hold upon her: and happy is every one that retaineth her.

Strive not with a man without cause, if he have done thee no harm.
Proverbs 3:13,18,30

He that is void of wisdom despiseth his neighbour: but a man of understanding holdeth his peace.

Proverbs 11:12

He that despiseth his neighbour sinneth: but he that hath mercy on the poor, happy is he.

He that is slow to wrath is of great understanding: but he that is hasty of spirit exalteth folly. *Proverbs 14:21,29*

A wicked man hardeneth his face: but as for the upright, He directeth his way. *Proverbs 21:29*

Let this mind be in you, which was also in Christ Jesus: *Philippians 2:5*

Follow peace with all men, and holiness, without which no man shall see the Lord: *Hebrews 12:14*

But the wisdom that is from above is first pure, then peaceable, gentle, and easy to be intreated, full of mercy and good fruits, without partiality, and without hypocrisy.

And the fruit of righteousness is sown in peace of them that make peace.

James 3:17,18

For he that will love life, and see good days, let him refrain his tongue from evil, and his lips that they speak no guile:

Let him eschew evil, and do good; let him seek peace, and ensue it.

1 Peter 3:10,11

8

PATIENT

Rest in the Lord, and wait patiently for Him: fret not thyself because of him who prospereth in his way, because of the man who bringeth wicked devices to pass. *Psalm 37:7*

A wrathful man stirreth up strife: but he that is slow to anger appeaseth strife. *Proverbs 15:18*

Better is the end of a thing than the beginning thereof: and the patient in spirit is better than the proud in spirit.

Be not hasty in thy spirit to be angry: for anger resteth in the bosom of fools. *Ecclesiastes 7:8,9*

It is good that a man should both

hope and quietly wait for the salvation of the Lord. *Lamentations 3:26*

But that on the good ground are they, which in an honest and good heart, having heard the word, keep it, and bring forth fruit with patience.
Luke 8:15

And He looked up, and saw the rich men casting their gifts into the treasury. *Luke 21:1*

And not only so, but we glory in tribulations also: knowing that tribulation worketh patience;

And patience, experience; and experience, hope: *Romans 5:3,4*

Rejoicing in hope; patient in tribulation; continuing instant in prayer; *Romans 12:12*

If then ye have judgments of things pertaining to this life, set them to judge who are least esteemed in the church.

I speak to your shame. Is it so,

that there is not a wise man among you? no, not one that shall be able to judge between his brethren?

1 Corinthians 6:4,5

But let patience have her perfect work, that ye may be perfect and entire, wanting nothing. *James 1:4*

And beside this, giving all diligence, add to your faith virtue; and to virtue knowledge;

And to knowledge temperance; and to temperance patience; and to patience godliness; *2 Peter 1:5,6*

9

SELF-CONTROLLED

And David said to Abishai, and to all his servants, Behold, my son, which came forth of my bowels, seeketh my life: how much more now may this Benjamite do it? let him alone, and let him curse; for the Lord hath bidden him. *2 Samuel 16:11*

Keep thy tongue from evil, and thy lips from speaking guile. *Psalm 34:13*

He that keepeth his mouth keepeth his life: but he that openeth wide his lips shall have destruction.
Proverbs 13:3

And as he reasoned of righteousness, temperance, and judgment to come, Felix trembled, and answered, Go thy way for this time; when I have a convenient season, I will call for thee.

Acts 24:25

Let not sin therefore reign in your mortal body, that ye should obey it in the lusts thereof. *Romans 6:12*

Paul, called to be an apostle of Jesus Christ through the will of God, and Sosthenes our brother,

1 Corinthians 1:1

But I keep under my body, and bring it into subjection: lest that by any means, when I have preached to others, I myself should be a castaway.

1 Corinthians 9:27

But the fruit of the Spirit is love, joy, peace, longsuffering, gentleness, goodness, faith, *Galatians 5:22*

Let your speech be alway with grace, seasoned with salt, that ye may know how ye ought to answer every man. *Colossians 4:6*

In meekness instructing those that oppose themselves; if God peradventure will give them repentance to the acknowledging of the truth;

2 Timothy 2:25

At my first answer no man stood with me, but all men forsook me: I pray God that it may not be laid to their charge. *2 Timothy 4:16*

If any man among you seem to be religious, and bridleth not his tongue, but deceiveth his own heart, this man's religion is vain. *James 1:26*

For in many things we offend all. If any man offend not in word, the same is a perfect man, and able also to bridle the whole body. *James 3:2*

Who are kept by the power of God through faith unto salvation ready to be revealed in the last time.

That the trial of your faith, being much more precious than of gold that perisheth, though it be tried with fire, might be found unto praise and honour and glory at the appearing of Jesus Christ: *1 Peter 1:5,7*

But let it be the hidden man of the heart, in that which is not corruptible, even the ornament of a meek and quiet spirit, which is in the sight of God of great price.

For after this manner in the old time the holy women also, who trusted in God, adorned themselves, being in subjection unto their own husbands:

For he that will love life, and see good days, let him refrain his tongue from evil, and his lips that they speak no guile: *1 Peter 3:4,5,10*

10

A GOOD LISTENER

And in all things that I have said unto you be circumspect: and make no mention of the name of other gods, neither let it be heard out of thy mouth.

Exodus 23:13

But take diligent heed to do the commandment and the law, which Moses the servant of the Lord charged you, to love the Lord your God, and to walk in all His ways, and to keep His commandments, and to cleave unto Him, and to serve Him with all your heart and with all your soul.

Joshua 22:5

The ear that heareth the reproof of life abideth among the wise.

Proverbs 15:31

Hearken unto Me now therefore, O ye children, and attend to the words of My mouth. *Proverbs 7:24*

He that answereth a matter before he heareth it, it is folly and shame unto him.

The heart of the prudent getteth knowledge; and the ear of the wise seeketh knowledge. *Proverbs 18:13,15*

The hearing ear, and the seeing eye, the Lord hath made even both of them. *Proverbs 20:12*

Apply thine heart unto instruction, and thine ears to the words of knowledge. *Proverbs 23:12*

As an earring of gold, and an ornament of fine gold, so is a wise reprover upon an obedient ear.

Proverbs 25:12

Take heed therefore how ye hear: for whosoever hath, to him shall be given; and whosoever hath not, from him shall be taken even that which he seemeth to have. *Luke 8:18*

Now it came to pass, as they went, that He entered into a certain village: and a certain woman named Martha received Him into her house.

And she had a sister called Mary, which also sat at Jesus' feet, and heard His word. *Luke 10:38,39*

And could not find what they might do: for all the people were very attentive to hear Him. *Luke 19:48*

Of Whom we have many things to say, and hard to be uttered, seeing ye are dull of hearing. *Hebrews 5:11*

Wherefore, my beloved brethren, let every man be swift to hear, slow to speak, slow to wrath:

For if any be a hearer of the word, and not a doer, he is like unto a man beholding his natural face in a glass:

For he beholdeth himself, and goeth his way, and straightway

forgetteth what manner of man he was.
James 1:19,23,24

He that hath an ear, let him hear what the Spirit saith unto the churches; He that overcometh shall not be hurt of the second death. *Revelation 2:11*

11

A TEACHER

And that thou mayest tell in the ears of thy son, and of thy son's son, what things I have wrought in Egypt, and my signs which I have done among them; that ye may know how that I am the Lord. *Exodus 10:2*

And it shall come to pass, when your children shall say unto you, What mean ye by this service? *Exodus 12:26*

Come, ye children, hearken unto Me: I will teach you the fear of the Lord. *Psalm 34:11*

I will open my mouth in a parable: I will utter dark sayings of old: *Psalm 78:2*

The just man walketh in his integrity: his children are blessed after him. *Proverbs 20:7*

Train up a child in the way he should go: and when he is old, he will not depart from it. *Proverbs 22:6*

Apply thine heart unto instruction, and thine ears to the words of knowledge.

Buy the truth, and sell it not; also wisdom, and instruction, and understanding. *Proverbs 23:12,23*

Whom shall He teach knowledge? and whom shall He make to understand doctrine? them that are weaned from the milk, and drawn from the breasts. *Isaiah 28:9*

12

APPROACHABLE

A soft answer turneth away wrath: but grievous words stir up anger.

Proverbs 15:1

He that is slow to anger is better than the mighty; and he that ruleth his spirit than he that taketh a city.

Proverbs 16:32

Blessed are the poor in spirit: for theirs is the kingdom of heaven.

Blessed are they that mourn: for they shall be comforted.

Blessed are the meek: for they shall inherit the earth.

Blessed are they which do hunger and thirst after righteousness: for they shall be filled.

Blessed are the merciful: for they shall obtain mercy.

Blessed are the pure in heart: for they shall see God.

Blessed are the peacemakers: for they shall be called the children of God.

Blessed are they which are persecuted for righteousness' sake: for theirs is the kingdom of heaven.

Blessed are ye, when men shall revile you, and persecute you, and shall say all manner of evil against you falsely, for My sake. *Matthew 5:3-11*

Take My yoke upon you, and learn of Me; for I am meek and lowly in heart: and ye shall find rest unto your souls.

Matthew 11:29

And He cometh to Bethsaida; and they bring a blind man unto Him, and besought Him to touch Him.

Mark 8:22

And He arose out of the synagogue, and entered into Simon's house. And Simon's wife's mother was taken with a great fever; and they besought Him for her. *Luke 4:38*

And when they came to Jesus, they besought Him instantly, saying, That He was worthy for whom He should do this:
Luke 7:4

When he heard that Jesus was come out of Judaea into Galilee, he went unto Him, and besought Him that He would come down, and heal his son: for he was at the point of death.
John 4:47

Let us therefore follow after the things which make for peace, and things wherewith one may edify another.
Romans 14:19

Charity suffereth long, and is kind; charity envieth not; charity vaunteth not itself, is not puffed up,

Doth not behave itself unseemly, seeketh not her own, is not easily provoked, thinketh no evil;

Rejoiceth not in iniquity, but rejoiceth in the truth;

Beareth all things, believeth all things, hopeth all things, endureth all things. *1 Corinthians 13:4-7*

Finally, be ye all of one mind, having compassion one of another, love as brethren, be pitiful, be courteous:
1 Peter 3:8

13

A GODLY EXAMPLE

For I have told him that I will judge his house for ever for the iniquity which he knoweth; because his sons made themselves vile, and he restrained them not. *1 Samuel 3:13*

And his sons walked not in his ways, but turned aside after lucre, and took bribes, and perverted judgment. *1 Samuel 8:3*

And his father had not displeased him at any time in saying, Why hast thou done so? and he also was a very goodly man; and his mother bare him after Absalom. *1 Kings 1:6*

And if thou wilt walk before Me, as David thy father walked, in integrity of heart, and in uprightness, to do according to all that I have commanded thee, and wilt keep My statutes and My judgments: *1 Kings 9:4*

And he did evil in the sight of the Lord, and walked in the way of his father, and in the way of his mother, and in the way of Jeroboam the son of Nebat, who made Israel to sin:

1 Kings 22:52

And the Lord was with Jehoshaphat, because he walked in the first ways of his father David, and sought not unto Baalim;

2 Chronicles 17:3

He also walked in the ways of the house of Ahab: for his mother was his counsellor to do wickedly.

2 Chronicles 22:3

And he did that which was right in the sight of the Lord, according to all that his father Amaziah did.

2 Chronicles 26:4

The rod and reproof give wisdom: but a child left to himself bringeth his mother to shame. *Proverbs 29:15*

But have walked after the imagination of their own heart, and after Baalim, which their fathers taught them: *Jeremiah 9:14*

All therefore whatsoever they bid you observe, that observe and do; but do not ye after their works: for they say, and do not. *Matthew 23:3*

Salt is good: but if the salt have lost his saltness, wherewith will ye season it? Have salt in yourselves, and have peace one with another.
Mark 9:50

For I have given you an example, that ye should do as I have done to you.
John 13:15

Now the God of patience and consolation grant you to be likeminded one toward another according to Christ Jesus: *Romans 15:5*

Let this mind be in you, which was also in Christ Jesus: *Philippians 2:5*

Masters, give unto your servants that which is just and equal; knowing that ye also have a Master in heaven.

Colossians 4:1

Let no man despise thy youth; but be thou an example of the believers, in word, in conversation, in charity, in spirit, in faith, in purity.

1 Timothy 4:12

When I call to remembrance the unfeigned faith that is in thee, which dwelt first in thy grandmother Lois, and thy mother Eunice; and I am persuaded that in thee also.

2 Timothy 1:5

In all things shewing thyself a pattern of good works: in doctrine shewing uncorruptness, gravity, sincerity, *Titus 2:7*

For even hereunto were ye called: because Christ also suffered for us, leaving us an example, that ye should follow His steps: *1 Peter 2:21*

14

A MAN OF INTEGRITY

For I know Him, that He will command His children and His household after Him, and they shall keep the way of the Lord, to do justice and judgment; that the Lord may bring upon Abraham that which He hath spoken of him. *Genesis 18:19*

Folly is joy to him that is destitute of wisdom: but a man of understanding walketh uprightly. *Proverbs 15:21*

Better is the poor that walketh in his integrity, than he that is perverse in his lips, and is a fool. *Proverbs 19:1*

The just man walketh in his integrity: his children are blessed after him. *Proverbs 20:7*

To do justice and judgment is more acceptable to the Lord than sacrifice.

Proverbs 21:3

A faithful man shall abound with blessings: but he that maketh haste to be rich shall not be innocent.

Proverbs 28:20

He that walketh righteously, and speaketh uprightly; he that despiseth the gain of oppressions, that shaketh his hands from holding of bribes, that stoppeth his ears from hearing of blood, and shutteth his eyes from seeing evil;

He shall dwell on high: his place of defence shall be the munitions of rocks: bread shall be given him; his waters shall be sure. *Isaiah 33:15,16*

And herein do I exercise myself, to have always a conscience void of offence toward God, and toward men.

Acts 24:16

Recompense to no man evil for evil. Provide things honest in the sight of all men. *Romans 12:17*

Wherefore ye must needs be subject, not only for wrath, but also for conscience sake.

Owe no man any thing, but to love one another: for he that loveth another hath fulfilled the law. *Romans 13:5,8*

Moreover it is required in stewards, that a man be found faithful. *1 Corinthians 4:2*

But have renounced the hidden things of dishonesty, not walking in craftiness, nor handling the word of God deceitfully; but by manifestation of the truth commending ourselves to every man's conscience in the sight of God. *2 Corinthians 4:2*

Providing for honest things, not only in the sight of the Lord, but also in the sight of men. *2 Corinthians 8:21*

Holding the mystery of the faith in a pure conscience. *1 Timothy 3:9*

Pray for us: for we trust we have a good conscience, in all things willing to live honestly. *Hebrews 13:18*

Having a good conscience; that, whereas they speak evil of you, as of evildoers, they may be ashamed that falsely accuse your good conversation in Christ. *1 Peter 3:16*

15

A LEADER

For I know Him, that He will command His children and His household after Him, and they shall keep the way of the Lord, to do justice and judgment; that the Lord may bring upon Abraham that which He hath spoken of him. *Genesis 18:19*

And he said unto them, Set your hearts unto all the words which I testify among you this day, which ye shall command your children to observe to do, all the words of this law.
Deuteronomy 32:46

Be strong, and quit yourselves like men, O ye Philistines, that ye be not servants unto the Hebrews, as they have been to you: quit yourselves like men, and fight. *1 Samuel 4:9*

The God of Israel said, the Rock of Israel spake to me, He that ruleth over men must be just, ruling in the fear of God. *2 Samuel 23:3*

For he sent letters into all the king's provinces, into every province according to the writing thereof, and to every people after their language, that every man should bear rule in his own house, and that it should be published according to the language of every people. *Esther 1:22*

Thou hast delivered me from the strivings of the people; and Thou hast made me the head of the heathen: a people whom I have not known shall serve me. *Psalm 18:43*

By me princes rule, and nobles, even all the judges of the earth.
Proverbs 8:16

The hand of the diligent shall bear rule: but the slothful shall be under tribute. *Proverbs 12:24*

And the Lord said, Who then is that faithful and wise steward, whom his lord shall make ruler over his household, to give them their portion of meat in due season?

Blessed is that servant, whom his lord when he cometh shall find so doing. *Luke 12:42,43*

And I say unto you, Make to yourselves friends of the mammon of unrighteousness; that, when ye fail, they may receive you into everlasting habitations. *Luke 16:9*

One that ruleth well his own house, having his children in subjection with all gravity;

For if a man know not how to rule his own house, how shall he take care of the church of God?

Let the deacons be the husbands of one wife, ruling their children and their own houses well. *1 Timothy 3:4,5,12*

These things command and teach.

Let no man despise thy youth; but be thou an example of the believers, in word, in conversation, in charity, in spirit, in faith, in purity.

1 Timothy 4:11,12

And the things that thou hast heard of me among many witnesses, the same commit thou to faithful men, who shall be able to teach others also.

2 Timothy 2:2

These things speak, and exhort, and rebuke with all authority. Let no man despise thee. *Titus 2:15*

Remember them which have the rule over you, who have spoken unto you the word of God: whose faith follow, considering the end of their conversation.

Obey them that have the rule over you, and submit yourselves: for they watch for your souls, as they that must give account, that they may do it with joy, and not with grief: for that is unprofitable for you.

Salute all them that have the rule over you, and all the saints. They of Italy salute you. *Hebrews 13:7,17,24*

16

A DISCIPLINARIAN

Thou shalt also consider in thine heart, that, as a man chasteneth his son, so the Lord thy God chasteneth thee. *Deuteronomy 8:5*

Behold, happy is the man whom God correcteth: therefore despise not thou the chastening of the Almighty: *Job 5:17*

Foolishness is bound in the heart of a child; but the rod of correction shall drive it far from him. *Proverbs 22:15*

Withhold not correction from the child: for if thou beatest him with the rod, he shall not die. *Proverbs 23:13*

Open rebuke is better than secret love.

Faithful are the wounds of a friend; but the kisses of an enemy are deceitful. *Proverbs 27:5,6*

Correct thy son, and he shall give thee rest; yea, he shall give delight unto thy soul. *Proverbs 29:17*

It is better to hear the rebuke of the wise, than for a man to hear the song of fools. *Ecclesiastes 7:5*

Take heed to yourselves: If thy brother trespass against thee, rebuke him; and if he repent, forgive him. *Luke 17:3*

17

A MOTIVATOR

Moreover as for me, God forbid that I should sin against the Lord in ceasing to pray for you: but I will teach you the good and the right way:

1 Samuel 12:23

Then I told them of the hand of my God which was good upon me; as also the king's words that he had spoken unto me. And they said, Let us rise up and build. So they strengthened their hands for this good work.

Nehemiah 2:18

A wise man will hear, and will increase learning; and a man of understanding shall attain unto wise counsels: *Proverbs 1:5*

Give instruction to a wise man,

and he will be yet wiser: teach a just man, and he will increase in learning.
Proverbs 9:9

He becometh poor that dealeth with a slack hand: but the hand of the diligent maketh rich.

He that gathereth in summer is a wise son: but he that sleepeth in harvest is a son that causeth shame.
Proverbs 10:4,5

A righteous man hateth lying: but a wicked man is loathsome, and cometh to shame. *Proverbs 13:5*

When the scorner is punished, the simple is made wise: and when the wise is instructed, he receiveth knowledge. *Proverbs 21:11*

Bow down thine ear, and hear the words of the wise, and apply thine heart unto my knowledge.

For it is a pleasant thing if thou keep them within thee; they shall withal be fitted in thy lips.

Proverbs 22:17,18

Apply thine heart unto instruction, and thine ears to the words of knowledge.

Buy the truth, and sell it not; also wisdom, and instruction, and understanding. *Proverbs 23:12,23*

Wherefore I put thee in remembrance that thou stir up the gift of God, which is in thee by the putting on of my hands. *2 Timothy 1:6*

18

A PROVIDER

The wicked borroweth, and payeth not again: but the righteous sheweth mercy, and giveth. *Psalm 37:21*

Like as a father pitieth his children, so the Lord pitieth them that fear Him. *Psalm 103:13*

Withhold not good from them to whom it is due, when it is in the power of thine hand to do it. *Proverbs 3:27*

He coveteth greedily all the day long: but the righteous giveth and spareth not. *Proverbs 21:26*

Is not this the fast that I have chosen? to loose the bands of wickedness, to undo the heavy burdens, and to let the oppressed go free, and that ye break every yoke?

Is it not to deal thy bread to the hungry, and that thou bring the poor that are cast out to thy house? when thou seest the naked, that thou cover him; and that thou hide not thyself from thine own flesh? *Isaiah 58:6,7*

Give to him that asketh thee, and from him that would borrow of thee turn not thou away. *Matthew 5:42*

Or what man is there of you, whom if his son ask bread, will he give him a stone?

Or if he ask a fish, will he give him a serpent?

If ye then, being evil, know how to give good gifts unto your children, how much more shall your Father which is in heaven give good things to them that ask Him? *Matthew 7:9-11*

And one of the multitude answered and said, Master, I have brought unto Thee my son, which hath a dumb spirit; *Mark 9:17*

So ought men to love their wives as their own bodies. He that loveth his wife loveth himself.

For no man ever yet hated his own flesh; but nourisheth and cherisheth it, even as the Lord the church:

Ephesians 5:28,29

But if any provide not for his own, and specially for those of his own house, he hath denied the faith, and is worse than an infidel. *1 Timothy 5:8*

If a brother or sister be naked, and destitute of daily food,

And one of you say unto them, Depart in peace, be ye warmed and filled; notwithstanding ye give them not those things which are needful to the body; what doth it profit?

James 2:15,16

But whoso hath this world's good, and seeth his brother have need, and shutteth up his bowels of compassion from him, how dwelleth the love of God in him? *1 John 3:17*

19

FAITHFUL TO HIS SPOUSE

And it came to pass after these things, that his master's wife cast her eyes upon Joseph; and she said, Lie with me.

But he refused, and said unto his master's wife, Behold, my master wotteth not what is with me in the house, and he hath committed all that he hath to my hand;

There is none greater in this house than I; neither hath he kept back any thing from me but thee, because thou art his wife: how then can I do this great wickedness, and sin against God?

And it came to pass, as she spake to Joseph day by day, that he hearkened not unto her, to lie by her, or to be with her.

And it came to pass about this time, that Joseph went into the house to do his business; and there was none of the men of the house there within.

And she caught him by his garment, saying, Lie with me: and he left his garment in her hand, and fled, and got him out. *Genesis 39:7-12*

Say unto wisdom, Thou art my sister; and call understanding thy kinswoman: *Proverbs 7:4*

But I say unto you, That whosoever looketh on a woman to lust after her hath committed adultery with her already in his heart. *Matthew 5:28*

And he said, That which cometh out of the man, that defileth the man.

For from within, out of the heart of men, proceed evil thoughts, adulteries, fornications, murders,

Thefts, covetousness, wickedness, deceit, lasciviousness, an evil eye, blasphemy, pride, foolishness:

All these evil things come from within, and defile the man.

Mark 7:20-23

Flee fornication. Every sin that a man doeth is without the body; but he that committeth fornication sinneth against his own body.

1 Corinthians 6:18

And the peace of God, which passeth all understanding, shall keep your hearts and minds through Christ Jesus.

Finally, brethren, whatsoever things are true, whatsoever things are honest, whatsoever things are just, whatsoever things are pure, whatsoever things are lovely, whatsoever things are of good report; if there be any virtue, and if there be any praise, think on these things. *Philippians 4:7,8*

Abstain from all appearance of evil. *1 Thessalonians 5:22*

Flee also youthful lusts: but follow righteousness, faith, charity, peace, with them that call on the Lord out of a pure heart. *2 Timothy 2:22*

Submit yourselves therefore to God. Resist the devil, and he will flee from you. *James 4:7*

20

CONSIDERATE

A friend loveth at all times, and a brother is born for adversity.
Proverbs 17:17

Ointment and perfume rejoice the heart: so doth the sweetness of a man's friend by hearty counsel. *Proverbs 27:9*

Therefore all things whatsoever ye would that men should do to you, do ye even so to them: for this is the law and the prophets. *Matthew 7:12*

A new commandment I give unto you, That ye love one another; as I have loved you, that ye also love one another.
John 13:34

I have shewed you all things, how that so labouring ye ought to support the weak, and to remember the words of the Lord Jesus, how He said, It is more blessed to give than to receive.

Acts 20:35

That is, that I may be comforted together with you by the mutual faith both of you and me. *Romans 1:12*

That I may come unto you with joy by the will of God, and may with you be refreshed. *Romans 15:32*

Greet Priscilla and Aquila my helpers in Christ Jesus:

Who have for my life laid down their own necks: unto whom not only I give thanks, but also all the churches of the Gentiles. *Romans 16:3,4*

I am glad of the coming of Stephanas and Fortunatus and Achaicus: for that which was lacking on your part they have supplied.

For they have refreshed my spirit and yours: therefore acknowledge ye them that are such.

1 Corinthians 16:17,18

Therefore we were comforted in your comfort: yea, and exceedingly the more joyed we for the joy of Titus, because his spirit was refreshed by you all. *2 Corinthians 7:13*

Bear ye one another's burdens, and so fulfil the law of Christ.

As we have therefore opportunity, let us do good unto all men, especially unto them who are of the household of faith. *Galatians 6:2,10*

Finally, be ye all of one mind, having compassion one of another, love as brethren, be pitiful, be courteous:

Not rendering evil for evil, or railing for railing: but contrariwise blessing; knowing that ye are thereunto called, that ye should inherit a blessing. *1 Peter 3:8,9*

Beloved, if God so loved us, we ought also to love one another. *1 John 4:11*

21

KIND

A good man sheweth favour, and lendeth: he will guide his affairs with discretion. *Psalm 112:5*

He that despiseth his neighbour sinneth: but he that hath mercy on the poor, happy is he. *Proverbs 14:21*

The desire of a man is his kindness: and a poor man is better than a liar. *Proverbs 19:22*

Thus speaketh the Lord of hosts, saying, Execute true judgment, and shew mercy and compassions every man to his brother:

And oppress not the widow, nor the fatherless, the stranger, nor the poor; and let none of you imagine evil against his brother in your heart.

Zechariah 7:9,10

Blessed are the merciful: for they shall obtain mercy.

Give to him that asketh thee, and from him that would borrow of thee turn not thou away. *Matthew 5:7,42*

Then shall the King say unto them on His right hand, Come, ye blessed of My Father, inherit the kingdom prepared for you from the foundation of the world:

For I was an hungred, and ye gave Me meat: I was thirsty, and ye gave Me drink: I was a stranger, and ye took Me in: *Matthew 25:34,35*

And if ye lend to them of whom ye hope to receive, what thank have ye? for sinners also lend to sinners, to receive as much again.

But love ye your enemies, and do good, and lend, hoping for nothing again; and your reward shall be great, and ye shall be the children of the Highest: for He is kind unto the unthankful and to the evil.

Luke 6:34,35

I have shewed you all things, how that so labouring ye ought to support the weak, and to remember the words of the Lord Jesus, how He said, It is more blessed to give than to receive.

Acts 20:35

Rejoice with them that do rejoice, and weep with them that weep.

Romans 12:15

We then that are strong ought to bear the infirmities of the weak, and not to please ourselves.

Let every one of us please his neighbour for his good to edification.

Now the God of patience and consolation grant you to be likeminded one toward another according to Christ Jesus:

Romans 15:1,2,5

Charity suffereth long, and is kind; charity envieth not; charity vaunteth not itself, is not puffed up,

Doth not behave itself unseemly, seeketh not her own, is not easily provoked, thinketh no evil;

Rejoiceth not in iniquity, but rejoiceth in the truth;

Beareth all things, believeth all things, hopeth all things, endureth all things. *1 Corinthians 13:4-7*

Brethren, if a man be overtaken in a fault, ye which are spiritual, restore such an one in the spirit of meekness; considering thyself, lest thou also be tempted.

Bear ye one another's burdens, and so fulfil the law of Christ.

Galatians 6:1,2

YOUR CHILDREN

22

WHEN YOUR CHILDREN BECOME REBELLIOUS TOWARD YOU

Better is the end of a thing than the beginning thereof: and the patient in spirit is better than the proud in spirit. *Ecclesiastes 7:8*

Many waters cannot quench love, neither can the floods drown it: if a man would give all the substance of his house for love, it would utterly be contemned. *Song of Solomon 8:7*

Can a woman forget her sucking child, that she should not have compassion on the son of her womb? yea, they may forget, yet will I not forget thee. *Isaiah 49:15*

Blessed are the poor in spirit: for theirs is the kingdom of heaven.

Blessed are they that mourn: for they shall be comforted.

Blessed are the meek: for they shall inherit the earth. *Matthew 5:3-5*

Doth not behave itself unseemly, seeketh not her own, is not easily provoked, thinketh no evil;

1 Corinthians 13:5

But the fruit of the Spirit is love, joy, peace, longsuffering, gentleness, goodness, faith,

Meekness, temperance: against such there is no law.

Let us not be desirous of vain glory, provoking one another, envying one another. *Galatians 5:22,23,26*

I therefore, the prisoner of the Lord, beseech you that ye walk worthy of the vocation wherewith ye are called,

With all lowliness and meekness, with longsuffering, forbearing one another in love;

Endeavouring to keep the unity of the Spirit in the bond of peace.

Be ye angry, and sin not: let not the sun go down upon your wrath:

Let no corrupt communication proceed out of your mouth, but that which is good to the use of edifying, that it may minister grace unto the hearers.

And grieve not the Holy Spirit of God, whereby ye are sealed unto the day of redemption.

Let all bitterness, and wrath, and anger, and clamour, and evil speaking, be put away from you, with all malice:

And be ye kind one to another, tenderhearted, forgiving one another, even as God for Christ's sake hath forgiven you. *Ephesians 4:1-3,26,29-32*

And, ye fathers, provoke not your children to wrath: but bring them up in the nurture and admonition of the Lord.

Wherefore take unto you the whole armour of God, that ye may be able to withstand in the evil day, and having done all, to stand.

Above all, taking the shield of faith, wherewith ye shall be able to quench all the fiery darts of the wicked.

Ephesians 6:4,13,16

23

WHEN YOUR CHILDREN BECOME REBELLIOUS TOWARD GOD

I will both lay me down in peace, and sleep: for Thou, Lord, only makest me dwell in safety. *Psalm 4:8*

O Lord my God, in Thee do I put my trust: save me from all them that persecute me, and deliver me:

Lest he tear my soul like a lion, rending it in pieces, while there is none to deliver. *Psalm 7:1,2*

Trust in the Lord, and do good; so shalt thou dwell in the land, and verily thou shalt be fed.

Delight thyself also in the Lord; and He shall give thee the desires of thine heart.

Commit thy way unto the Lord; trust also in Him; and He shall bring it to pass.

And He shall bring forth thy righteousness as the light, and thy judgment as the noonday.

Rest in the Lord, and wait patiently for Him: fret not thyself because of him who prospereth in his way, because of the man who bringeth wicked devices to pass.

Cease from anger, and forsake wrath: fret not thyself in any wise to do evil. *Psalm 37:3-8*

Recompense to no man evil for evil. Provide things honest in the sight of all men. *Romans 12:17*

Forbearing one another, and forgiving one another, if any man have a quarrel against any: even as Christ forgave you, so also do ye.

Colossians 3:13

For Demas hath forsaken me, having loved this present world, and is departed unto Thessalonica; Crescens to Galatia, Titus unto Dalmatia.

2 Timothy 4:10

At my first answer no man stood with me, but all men forsook me: I pray God that it may not be laid to their charge.

Notwithstanding the Lord stood with me, and strengthened me; that by me the preaching might be fully known, and that all the Gentiles might hear: and I was delivered out of the mouth of the lion.

And the Lord shall deliver me from every evil work, and will preserve me unto His heavenly kingdom: to Whom be glory for ever and ever. Amen.

2 Timothy 4:16-18

For consider Him that endured such contradiction of sinners against Himself, lest ye be wearied and faint in your minds. *Hebrews 12:3*

Let your conversation be without covetousness; and be content with such things as ye have: for He hath said, I will never leave thee, nor forsake thee.

So that we may boldly say, The Lord is my helper, and I will not fear what man shall do unto me.

Hebrews 13:5,6

24

When Your Children Become Lazy And Disinterested

Moreover as for me, God forbid that I should sin against the Lord in ceasing to pray for you: but I will teach you the good and the right way:

1 Samuel 12:23

Then I told them of the hand of my God which was good upon me; as also the king's words that he had spoken unto me. And they said, Let us rise up and build. So they strengthened their hands for this good work.

Nehemiah 2:18

A wise man will hear, and will increase learning; and a man of understanding shall attain unto wise counsels: *Proverbs 1:5*

By much slothfulness the building decayeth; and through idleness of the hands the house droppeth through. *Ecclesiastes 10:18*

Who is wise, and he shall understand these things? prudent, and he shall know them? for the ways of the Lord are right, and the just shall walk in them: but the transgressors shall fall therein. *Hosea 14:9*

Jesus saith unto him, Rise, take up thy bed, and walk. *John 5:8*

Not slothful in business; fervent in spirit; serving the Lord; *Romans 12:11*

Wherefore he saith, Awake thou that sleepest, and arise from the dead, and Christ shall give thee light. *Ephesians 5:14*

Walk in wisdom toward them that are without, redeeming the time. *Colossians 4:5*

These things command and teach.

1 Timothy 4:11

Looking unto Jesus the author and finisher of our faith; who for the joy that was set before Him endured the cross, despising the shame, and is set down at the right hand of the throne of God.

Hebrews 12:2

25

When Your Children Begin To Withdraw From You

Thou shalt also decree a thing, and it shall be established unto thee: and the light shall shine upon thy ways.

When men are cast down, then thou shalt say, There is lifting up; and He shall save the humble person.

Job 22:28,29

But Thou, O Lord, art a shield for me; my glory, and the lifter up of mine head. *Psalm 3:3*

For Thou wilt light my candle: the Lord my God will enlighten my darkness. *Psalm 18:28*

My foot standeth in an even place: in the congregations will I bless the

Lord. *Psalm 26:12*

I will lift up mine eyes unto the hills, from whence cometh my help.

My help cometh from the Lord, which made heaven and earth.

He will not suffer thy foot to be moved: He that keepeth thee will not slumber. *Psalm 121:1-3*

Hear me speedily, O Lord: my spirit faileth: hide not Thy face from me, lest I be like unto them that go down into the pit. *Psalm 143:7*

Blessed are ye, when men shall revile you, and persecute you, and shall say all manner of evil against you falsely, for My sake. *Matthew 5:11*

And the brother shall deliver up the brother to death, and the father the child: and the children shall rise up against their parents, and cause them to be put to death. *Matthew 10:21*

My little children, let us not love in

word, neither in tongue; but in deed and in truth.

And hereby we know that we are of the truth, and shall assure our hearts before Him.

For if our heart condemn us, God is greater than our heart, and knoweth all things.

Beloved, if our heart condemn us not, then have we confidence toward God.

And whatsoever we ask, we receive of Him, because we keep His commandments, and do those things that are pleasing in His sight. *1 John 3:18-22*

Ye are of God, little children, and have overcome them: because greater is He that is in you, than he that is in the world. *1 John 4:4*

26

WHEN YOUR CHILDREN ENCOUNTER PEER PRESSURE

If thy brother, the son of thy mother, or thy son, or thy daughter, or the wife of thy bosom, or thy friend, which is as thine own soul, entice thee secretly, saying, Let us go and serve other gods, which thou hast not known, thou, nor thy fathers;

Thou shalt not consent unto him, nor hearken unto him; neither shall thine eye pity him, neither shalt thou spare, neither shalt thou conceal him:

Deuteronomy 13:6,8

He that putteth not out his money to usury, nor taketh reward against the innocent. He that doeth these things shall never be moved. *Psalm 15:5*

Who shall ascend into the hill of the Lord? or who shall stand in His holy place?

He that hath clean hands, and a pure heart; who hath not lifted up his soul unto vanity, nor sworn deceitfully.

He shall receive the blessing from the Lord, and righteousness from the God of his salvation. *Psalm 24:3-5*

My son, if sinners entice thee, consent thou not.

If they say, Come with us, let us lay wait for blood, let us lurk privily for the innocent without cause:

Let us swallow them up alive as the grave; and whole, as those that go down into the pit:

We shall find all precious substance, we shall fill our houses with spoil:

Cast in thy lot among us; let us all have one purse:

My son, walk not thou in the way with them; refrain thy foot from their path: *Proverbs 1:10-15*

Keep thy heart with all diligence; for out of it are the issues of life.

Put away from thee a froward mouth, and perverse lips put far from thee.

Let thine eyes look right on, and let thine eyelids look straight before thee.

Ponder the path of thy feet, and let all thy ways be established.

Turn not to the right hand nor to the left: remove thy foot from evil.

Proverbs 4:23-27

He that walketh righteously, and speaketh uprightly; he that despiseth the gain of oppressions, that shaketh his hands from holding of bribes, that stoppeth his ears from hearing of blood, and shutteth his eyes from seeing evil;

He shall dwell on high: his place of defence shall be the munitions of rocks: bread shall be given him; his waters shall be sure. *Isaiah 33:15,16*

Let no man say when he is tempted, I am tempted of God: for God cannot be tempted with evil, neither tempteth He any man:

But every man is tempted, when he is drawn away of his own lust, and enticed.

Then when lust hath conceived, it bringeth forth sin: and sin, when it is finished, bringeth forth death.

Do not err, my beloved brethren.

James 1:13-16

27

WHEN YOUR CHILDREN ARE JEALOUS OF YOUR ATTENTION SHOWN TO OTHERS

The Lord also will be a refuge for the oppressed, a refuge in times of trouble. *Psalm 9:9*

Plead my cause, O Lord, with them that strive with me: fight against them that fight against me.

Take hold of shield and buckler, and stand up for mine help.

Psalm 35:1,2

I can do all things through Christ which strengtheneth me.

Philippians 4:13

At my first answer no man stood with me, but all men forsook me: I pray God that it may not be laid to their charge.

Notwithstanding the Lord stood with me, and strengthened me; that by me the preaching might be fully known, and that all the Gentiles might hear: and I was delivered out of the mouth of the lion. *2 Timothy 4:16,17*

For in that He Himself hath suffered being tempted, He is able to succour them that are tempted.

Hebrews 2:18

Who through faith subdued kingdoms, wrought righteousness, obtained promises, stopped the mouths of lions,

Quenched the violence of fire, escaped the edge of the sword, out of weakness were made strong, waxed valiant in fight, turned to flight the armies of the aliens.

And others had trial of cruel mockings and scourgings, yea,

moreover of bonds and imprisonment:
Hebrews 11:33,34,36

My brethren, count it all joy when ye fall into divers temptations;
Knowing this, that the trying of your faith worketh patience.
James 1:2,3

Wherein ye greatly rejoice, though now for a season, if need be, ye are in heaviness through manifold temptations:
That the trial of your faith, being much more precious than of gold that perisheth, though it be tried with fire, might be found unto praise and honour and glory at the appearing of Jesus Christ: *1 Peter 1:6,7*

28

WHEN YOUR CHILDREN ACQUIRE A POOR SELF-IMAGE

Thou shalt not oppress an hired servant that is poor and needy, whether he be of thy brethren, or of thy strangers that are in thy land within thy gates: *Deuteronomy 24:14*

Heaviness in the heart of man maketh it stoop: but a good word maketh it glad. *Proverbs 12:25*

A man hath joy by the answer of his mouth: and a word spoken in due season, how good is it!

The light of the eyes rejoiceth the heart: and a good report maketh the bones fat. *Proverbs 15:23,30*

He that hath a bountiful eye shall be blessed; for he giveth of his bread to the poor. *Proverbs 22:9*

A word fitly spoken is like apples of gold in pictures of silver.
Proverbs 25:11

A fool uttereth all his mind: but a wise man keepeth it in till afterwards.
Proverbs 29:11

Laying up in store for themselves a good foundation against the time to come, that they may lay hold on eternal life. *1 Timothy 6:19*

But to do good and to communicate forget not: for with such sacrifices God is well pleased. *Hebrews 13:16*

29

WHEN YOUR CHILDREN BECOME UNFORGIVING TOWARD YOU

For the Lord thy God is a merciful God; He will not forsake thee, neither destroy thee, nor forget the covenant of thy fathers which He sware unto them.
Deuteronomy 4:31

Be strong and of a good courage, fear not, nor be afraid of them: for the Lord thy God, He it is that doth go with thee; He will not fail thee, nor forsake thee. *Deuteronomy 31:6*

For the Lord will not forsake His people for His great name's sake: because it hath pleased the Lord to make you His people. *1 Samuel 12:22*

I have been young, and now am old; yet have I not seen the righteous

forsaken, nor his seed begging bread.
Psalm 37:25

Can a woman forget her sucking child, that she should not have compassion on the son of her womb? yea, they may forget, yet will I not forget thee. *Isaiah 49:15*

Behold, I have graven thee upon the palms of My hands; thy walls are continually before Me. *Isaiah 49:16*

Thou shalt no more be termed Forsaken; neither shall thy land any more be termed Desolate: but thou shalt be called Hephzibah, and thy land Beulah: for the Lord delighteth in thee, and thy land shall be married.
Isaiah 62:4

Teaching them to observe all things whatsoever I have commanded you: and, lo, I am with you alway, even unto the end of the world. Amen.
Matthew 28:20

Casting all your care upon Him; for He careth for you. *1 Peter 5:7*

30

When Your Children Become Quarrelsome

Thou shalt be hid from the scourge of the tongue: neither shalt thou be afraid of destruction when it cometh.
Job 5:21

Thou shalt hide them in the secret of Thy presence from the pride of man: Thou shalt keep them secretly in a pavilion from the strife of tongues.
Psalm 31:20

Keep thy tongue from evil, and thy lips from speaking guile.

Depart from evil, and do good; seek peace, and pursue it. *Psalm 34:13,14*

He that is void of wisdom despiseth his neighbour: but a man of

understanding holdeth his peace.
Proverbs 11:12

Only by pride cometh contention: but with the well advised is wisdom.
Proverbs 13:10

He that is slow to wrath is of great understanding: but he that is hasty of spirit exalteth folly. *Proverbs 14:29*

A wrathful man stirreth up strife: but he that is slow to anger appeaseth strife. *Proverbs 15:18*

The beginning of strife is as when one letteth out water: therefore leave off contention, before it be meddled with.

He that hath knowledge spareth his words: and a man of understanding is of an excellent spirit.

Even a fool, when he holdeth his peace, is counted wise: and he that shutteth his lips is esteemed a man of understanding. *Proverbs 17:14,27,28*

A fool's lips enter into contention, and his mouth calleth for strokes.

The lot causeth contentions to cease, and parteth between the mighty.

A brother offended is harder to be won than a strong city: and their contentions are like the bars of a castle.

Proverbs 18:6,18,19

Who is a wise man and endued with knowledge among you? let him shew out of a good conversation his works with meekness of wisdom.

But if ye have bitter envying and strife in your hearts, glory not, and lie not against the truth.

This wisdom descendeth not from above, but is earthly, sensual, devilish.

For where envying and strife is, there is confusion and every evil work.

But the wisdom that is from above is first pure, then peaceable, gentle, and easy to be intreated, full of mercy and good fruits, without partiality, and without hypocrisy.

And the fruit of righteousness is sown in peace of them that make peace.

James 3:13-18

31

When Your Children Must Cope With Parental Disharmony

After these things the word of the Lord came unto Abram in a vision, saying, Fear not, Abram: I am thy shield, and thy exceeding great reward.
Genesis 15:1

Happy art thou, O Israel: Who is like unto thee, O people saved by the Lord, the shield of thy help, and Who is the sword of thy excellency! and thine enemies shall be found liars unto thee; and thou shalt tread upon their high places. *Deuteronomy 33:29*

And he said, The Lord is my rock, and my fortress, and my deliverer;

The God of my rock; in Him will I

trust: He is my shield, and the horn of my salvation, my high tower, and my refuge, my saviour; Thou savest me from violence.

I will call on the Lord, Who is worthy to be praised: so shall I be saved from mine enemies.

2 Samuel 22:2-4

He shall cover thee with His feathers, and under His wings shalt thou trust: His truth shall be thy shield and buckler. *Psalm 91:4*

Ye that fear the Lord, trust in the Lord: He is their help and their shield.

Psalm 115:11

Thou art my hiding place and my shield: I hope in Thy word.

Psalm 119:114

Blessed be the Lord my strength, which teacheth my hands to war, and my fingers to fight: *Psalm 144:1*

My goodness, and my fortress; my

high tower, and my deliverer; my shield, and He in Whom I trust; Who subdueth my people under me. *Psalm 144:2*

Then shalt thou walk in thy way safely, and thy foot shall not stumble.

When thou liest down, thou shalt not be afraid: yea, thou shalt lie down, and thy sleep shall be sweet.

Proverbs 3:23,24

32

When Your Children Become Sick

And said, If thou wilt diligently hearken to the voice of the Lord thy God, and wilt do that which is right in His sight, and wilt give ear to His commandments, and keep all His statutes, I will put none of these diseases upon thee, which I have brought upon the Egyptians: for I am the Lord that healeth thee. *Exodus 15:26*

But if from thence thou shalt seek the Lord thy God, thou shalt find Him, if thou seek Him with all thy heart and with all thy soul.

When thou art in tribulation, and all these things are come upon thee, even in the latter days, if thou turn to the Lord thy God, and shalt be obedient unto His voice;

For the Lord thy God is a merciful God; He will not forsake thee, neither destroy thee, nor forget the covenant of thy fathers which He sware unto them.
Deuteronomy 4:29-31

Who forgiveth all thine iniquities; Who healeth all thy diseases;
Who redeemeth thy life from destruction; Who crowneth thee with lovingkindness and tender mercies;
Who satisfieth thy mouth with good things; so that thy youth is renewed like the eagle's. *Psalm 103:3-5*

Let, I pray thee, Thy merciful kindness be for my comfort, according to Thy word unto Thy servant.
Let Thy tender mercies come unto me, that I may live: for Thy law is my delight. *Psalm 119:76,77*

Surely He hath borne our griefs, and carried our sorrows: yet we did esteem Him stricken, smitten of God, and afflicted.
But He was wounded for our trans-

gressions, He was bruised for our iniquities: the chastisement of our peace was upon Him; and with His stripes we are healed. *Isaiah 53:4,5*

And Jesus saith unto him, I will come and heal him. *Matthew 8:7*

Humble yourselves in the sight of the Lord, and He shall lift you up.
James 4:10

Is any among you afflicted? let him pray. Is any merry? let him sing psalms.

Is any sick among you? let him call for the elders of the church; and let them pray over him, anointing him with oil in the name of the Lord:

And the prayer of faith shall save the sick, and the Lord shall raise him up; and if he have committed sins, they shall be forgiven him.

Confess your faults one to another, and pray one for another, that ye may be healed. The effectual fervent prayer of a righteous man availeth much.

Elias was a man subject to like passions as we are, and he prayed earnestly that it might not rain: and it rained not on the earth by the space of three years and six months.

And he prayed again, and the heaven gave rain, and the earth brought forth her fruit. *James 5:13-18*

33

When Your Children Have Thoughts Of Suicide

For the needy shall not alway be forgotten: the expectation of the poor shall not perish for ever. *Psalm 9:18*

Be of good courage, and He shall strengthen your heart, all ye that hope in the Lord. *Psalm 31:24*

Behold, the eye of the Lord is upon them that fear Him, upon them that hope in His mercy;

Let Thy mercy, O Lord, be upon us, according as we hope in Thee.

Psalm 33:18,22

Hope deferred maketh the heart sick: but when the desire cometh, it is a tree of life. *Proverbs 13:12*

For surely there is an end; and thine expectation shall not be cut off.
Proverbs 23:18

Behold, God is my salvation; I will trust, and not be afraid: for the Lord Jehovah is my strength and my song; He also is become my salvation.

Therefore with joy shall ye draw water out of the wells of salvation.
Isaiah 12:2,3

Blessed is the man that trusteth in the Lord, and whose hope the Lord is.
Jeremiah 17:7

This I recall to my mind, therefore have I hope.

The Lord is my portion, saith my soul; therefore will I hope in Him.

It is good that a man should both hope and quietly wait for the salvation of the Lord. *Lamentations 3:21,24,26*

Peace I leave with you, My peace I give unto you: not as the world giveth, give I unto you. Let not your heart be troubled, neither let it be afraid.

John 14:27

Who against hope believed in hope, that He might become the father of many nations, according to that which was spoken, So shall thy seed be.

Romans 4:18

Rejoicing in hope; patient in tribulation; continuing instant in prayer; *Romans 12:12*

Now the God of hope fill you with all joy and peace in believing, that ye may abound in hope, through the power of the Holy Ghost. *Romans 15:13*

And now abideth faith, hope, charity, these three; but the greatest of these is charity. *1 Corinthians 13:13*

But rejoice, inasmuch as ye are partakers of Christ's sufferings; that, when His glory shall be revealed, ye may be glad also with exceeding joy.

1 Peter 4:13

34

WHEN YOUR CHILDREN DO NOT WANT TO ATTEND CHURCH

And I say also unto thee, That thou art Peter, and upon this rock I will build my church; and the gates of hell shall not prevail against it. *Matthew 16:18*

And Jesus said unto them, Because of your unbelief: for verily I say unto you, If ye have faith as a grain of mustard seed, ye shall say unto this mountain, Remove hence to yonder place; and it shall remove; and nothing shall be impossible unto you.

Matthew 17:20

And Jesus answering saith unto them, Have faith in God. *Mark 11:22*

Peace I leave with you, My peace I give unto you: not as the world giveth, give I unto you. Let not your heart be troubled, neither let it be afraid.

John 14:27

For I am the least of the apostles, that am not meet to be called an apostle, because I persecuted the church of God. *1 Corinthians 15:9*

Who comforteth us in all our tribulation, that we may be able to comfort them which are in any trouble, by the comfort wherewith we ourselves are comforted of God.

2 Corinthians 1:4

Which is not another; but there be some that trouble you, and would pervert the gospel of Christ.

For ye have heard of my conversation in time past in the Jews' religion, how that beyond measure I persecuted the church of God, and wasted it:

Galatians 1:7,13

Husbands, love your wives, even as Christ also loved the church, and gave Himself for it;

That He might present it to Himself a glorious church, not having spot, or wrinkle, or any such thing; but that it should be holy and without blemish. *Ephesians 5:25,27*

Being confident of this very thing, that He which hath begun a good work in you will perform it until the day of Jesus Christ: *Philippians 1:6*

35

WHEN YOUR CHILDREN ARE HEARTBROKEN BY DIVORCE

But if from thence thou shalt seek the Lord thy God, thou shalt find Him, if thou seek Him with all thy heart and with all thy soul.

When thou art in tribulation, and all these things are come upon thee, even in the latter days, if thou turn to the Lord thy God, and shalt be obedient unto His voice;

For the Lord thy God is a merciful God; He will not forsake thee, neither destroy thee, nor forget the covenant of thy fathers which He sware unto them.

Deuteronomy 4:29-31

Be strong and of a good courage,

fear not, nor be afraid of them: for the Lord thy God, He it is that doth go with thee; He will not fail thee, nor forsake thee. *Deuteronomy 31:6*

Likewise the Spirit also helpeth our infirmities: for we know not what we should pray for as we ought: but the Spirit itself maketh intercession for us with groanings which cannot be uttered. *Romans 8:26*

And grieve not the Holy Spirit of God, whereby ye are sealed unto the day of redemption.

Let all bitterness, and wrath, and anger, and clamour, and evil speaking, be put away from you, with all malice:

And be ye kind one to another, tenderhearted, forgiving one another, even as God for Christ's sake hath forgiven you. *Ephesians 4:30-32*

Finally, my brethren, be strong in the Lord, and in the power of His might.

Put on the whole armour of God, that ye may be able to stand against the wiles of the devil.

Praying always with all prayer and supplication in the Spirit, and watching thereunto with all perseverance and supplication for all saints;

Ephesians 6:10,11,18

Be careful for nothing; but in every thing by prayer and supplication with thanksgiving let your requests be made known unto God.

And the peace of God, which passeth all understanding, shall keep your hearts and minds through Christ Jesus.

I can do all things through Christ which strengtheneth me.

But my God shall supply all your need according to His riches in glory by Christ Jesus. *Philippians 4:6,7,13,19*

Let your conversation be without covetousness; and be content with such things as ye have: for He hath said, I will never leave thee, nor forsake thee.

Hebrews 13:5

YOUR WIFE

36

WHEN YOUR WIFE SEEMS UNSUPPORTIVE OF YOUR DREAMS AND GOALS

Lord, how are they increased that trouble me! many are they that rise up against me.

Many there be which say of my soul, There is no help for him in God.

But Thou, O Lord, art a shield for me; my glory, and the lifter up of mine head. *Psalm 3:1-3*

Have mercy upon me, O Lord; for I am weak: O Lord, heal me; for my bones are vexed. *Psalm 6:2*

The Lord is my light and my salvation; whom shall I fear? the Lord is the strength of my life; of whom shall I be afraid?

Though an host should encamp against me, my heart shall not fear: though war should rise against me, in this will I be confident.

I had fainted, unless I had believed to see the goodness of the Lord in the land of the living.

Wait on the Lord: be of good courage, and He shall strengthen thine heart: wait, I say, on the Lord.

Psalm 27:1,3,13,14

For Thou art my rock and my fortress; therefore for Thy name's sake lead me, and guide me.

Pull me out of the net that they have laid privily for me: for Thou art my strength. *Psalm 31:3,4*

Thou art my hiding place; Thou shalt preserve me from trouble; Thou shalt compass me about with songs of deliverance. *Psalm 32:7*

I can do all things through Christ which strengtheneth me.

But my God shall supply all your need according to His riches in glory by Christ Jesus. *Philippians 4:13,19*

Put on therefore, as the elect of God, holy and beloved, bowels of mercies, kindness, humbleness of mind, meekness, longsuffering;

Forbearing one another, and forgiving one another, if any man have a quarrel against any: even as Christ forgave you, so also do ye.

And above all these things put on charity, which is the bond of perfectness.

And let the peace of God rule in your hearts, to the which also ye are called in one body; and be ye thankful.

Colossians 3:12-15

Confess your faults one to another, and pray one for another, that ye may be healed. The effectual fervent prayer of a righteous man availeth much.

James 5:16

37

When Your Wife Disagrees With You About The Children's Discipline

Lord, who shall abide in Thy tabernacle? who shall dwell in Thy holy hill?

He that walketh uprightly, and worketh righteousness, and speaketh the truth in his heart. *Psalm 15:1,2*

Keep thy tongue from evil, and thy lips from speaking guile. *Psalm 34:13*

The mouth of the righteous speaketh wisdom, and his tongue talketh of judgment. *Psalm 37:30*

I said, I will take heed to my ways, that I sin not with my tongue: I will keep my mouth with a bridle, while the wicked is before me. *Psalm 39:1*

The heart of the righteous studieth to answer: but the mouth of the wicked poureth out evil things. *Proverbs 15:28*

A fool uttereth all his mind: but a wise man keepeth it in till afterwards.

Seest thou a man that is hasty in his words? there is more hope of a fool than of him. *Proverbs 29:11,20*

But let your communication be, Yea, yea; Nay, nay: for whatsoever is more than these cometh of evil.
Matthew 5:37

A good man out of the good treasure of the heart bringeth forth good things: and an evil man out of the evil treasure bringeth forth evil things.
Matthew 12:35

And be renewed in the spirit of your mind;

Let no corrupt communication proceed out of your mouth, but that which is good to the use of edifying, that it may minister grace unto the hearers.

Let all bitterness, and wrath, and anger, and clamour, and evil speaking, be put away from you, with all malice:

Ephesians 4:23,29,31

Wherefore be ye not unwise, but understanding what the will of the Lord is.

Submitting yourselves one to another in the fear of God.

Wives, submit yourselves unto your own husbands, as unto the Lord.

For the husband is the head of the wife, even as Christ is the head of the church: and He is the saviour of the body.

Husbands, love your wives, even as Christ also loved the church, and gave Himself for it;

So ought men to love their wives as their own bodies. He that loveth his wife loveth himself.

Ephesians 5:17,21-23,25,28

Not rendering evil for evil, or railing for railing: but contrariwise blessing; knowing that ye are thereunto called, that ye should inherit a blessing.

For he that will love life, and see good days, let him refrain his tongue from evil, and his lips that they speak no guile:

Let him eschew evil, and do good; let him seek peace, and ensue it.

1 Peter 3:9-11

38

WHEN YOUR WIFE SEEMS OVERLY CRITICAL OR ABUSIVE

I said, I will take heed to my ways, that I sin not with my tongue: I will keep my mouth with a bridle, while the wicked is before me. *Psalm 39:1*

The lip of truth shall be established for ever: but a lying tongue is but for a moment. *Proverbs 12:19*

A soft answer turneth away wrath: but grievous words stir up anger. *Proverbs 15:1*

And lead us not into temptation, but deliver us from evil: For Thine is the kingdom, and the power, and the glory, for ever. Amen. *Matthew 6:13*

Recompense to no man evil for evil. Provide things honest in the sight of all men.

If it be possible, as much as lieth in you, live peaceably with all men.

Dearly beloved, avenge not yourselves, but rather give place unto wrath: for it is written, Vengeance is Mine; I will repay, saith the Lord.

Therefore if thine enemy hunger, feed him; if he thirst, give him drink: for in so doing thou shalt heap coals of fire on his head.

Be not overcome of evil, but overcome evil with good.

Romans 12:17-21

And labour, working with our own hands: being reviled, we bless; being persecuted, we suffer it:

1 Corinthians 4:12

Charity suffereth long, and is kind; charity envieth not; charity vaunteth not itself, is not puffed up,

Doth not behave itself unseemly, seeketh not her own, is not easily provoked, thinketh no evil;

Rejoiceth not in iniquity, but rejoiceth in the truth;

Beareth all things, believeth all things, hopeth all things, endureth all things. *1 Corinthians 13:4-7*

See that none render evil for evil unto any man; but ever follow that which is good, both among yourselves, and to all men. *1 Thessalonians 5:15*

Follow peace with all men, and holiness, without which no man shall see the Lord: *Hebrews 12:14*

Who, when He was reviled, reviled not again; when He suffered, He threatened not; but committed Himself to Him that judgeth righteously:
1 Peter 2:23

39

WHEN YOUR WIFE SEEMS JEALOUS OR OVERPROTECTIVE

And these words, which I command thee this day, shall be in thine heart:

And thou shalt write them upon the posts of thy house, and on thy gates.

Deuteronomy 6:6,9

And he led them forth by the right way, that they might go to a city of habitation. *Psalm 107:7*

Peace be within thy walls, and prosperity within thy palaces.

Psalm 122:7

Lo, children are an heritage of the

Lord: and the fruit of the womb is his reward.

As arrows are in the hand of a mighty man; so are children of the youth. *Psalm 127:3,4*

Now the God of patience and consolation grant you to be likeminded one toward another according to Christ Jesus:

That ye may with one mind and one mouth glorify God, even the Father of our Lord Jesus Christ.

Wherefore receive ye one another, as Christ also received us to the glory of God. *Romans 15:5-7*

If any man defile the temple of God, him shall God destroy; for the temple of God is holy, which temple ye are. *1 Corinthians 3:17*

Casting all your care upon Him; for He careth for you. *1 Peter 5:7*

Beloved, if our heart condemn us not, then have we confidence toward

God. *1 John 3:21*

And this is the confidence that we have in Him, that, if we ask any thing according to His will, He heareth us:

And if we know that He hear us, whatsoever we ask, we know that we have the petitions that we desired of Him. *1 John 5:14,15*

40

WHEN YOUR WIFE HAS RESPONSIBILITIES AWAY FROM HOME

Wait on the Lord: be of good courage, and He shall strengthen thine heart: wait, I say, on the Lord.

Psalm 27:14

Be of good courage, and He shall strengthen your heart, all ye that hope in the Lord. *Psalm 31:24*

Strengthen ye the weak hands, and confirm the feeble knees.

Say to them that are of a fearful heart, Be strong, fear not: behold, your God will come with vengeance, even God with a recompence; He will come and save you. *Isaiah 35:3,4*

Fear thou not; for I am with thee: be not dismayed; for I am thy God: I will strengthen thee; yea, I will help thee; yea, I will uphold thee with the right hand of My righteousness.

Isaiah 41:10

Strengthened with all might, according to His glorious power, unto all patience and longsuffering with joyfulness; *Colossians 1:11*

For God hath not given us the spirit of fear; but of power, and of love, and of a sound mind. *2 Timothy 1:7*

Thou therefore, my son, be strong in the grace that is in Christ Jesus.

2 Timothy 2:1

Let us therefore come boldly unto the throne of grace, that we may obtain mercy, and find grace to help in time of need. *Hebrews 4:16*

Through faith also Sara herself received strength to conceive seed, and was delivered of a child when she was past age, because she judged Him faithful who had promised.

Quenched the violence of fire, escaped the edge of the sword, out of weakness were made strong, waxed valiant in fight, turned to flight the armies of the aliens. *Hebrews 11:11,34*

So that we may boldly say, The Lord is my helper, and I will not fear what man shall do unto me.

Hebrews 13:6

But the God of all grace, who hath called us unto His eternal glory by Christ Jesus, after that ye have suffered a while, make you perfect, stablish, strengthen, settle you.

1 Peter 5:10

YOUR WORK

41

WHEN YOU ARE ACCUSED OF BEING A WORKAHOLIC

And Moses said unto them, Stand still, and I will hear what the Lord will command concerning you.

Numbers 9:8

And as they were going down to the end of the city, Samuel said to Saul, Bid the servant pass on before us, and he passed on, but stand thou still a while, that I may shew thee the word of God. *1 Samuel 9:27*

Now therefore stand still, that I

may reason with you before the Lord of all the righteous acts of the Lord, which He did to you and to your fathers.

1 Samuel 12:7

And the king said unto him, Turn aside, and stand here. And he turned aside, and stood still. *2 Samuel 18:30*

And after the earthquake a fire; but the Lord was not in the fire: and after the fire a still small voice.

1 Kings 19:12

And the work of righteousness shall be peace; and the effect of righteousness quietness and assurance for ever.

And My people shall dwell in a peaceable habitation, and in sure dwellings, and in quiet resting places;

Isaiah 32:17,18

O Lord, I know that the way of man is not in himself: it is not in man that walketh to direct his steps.

Jeremiah 10:23

But Martha was cumbered about much serving, and came to Him, and said, Lord, dost Thou not care that my sister hath left me to serve alone? bid her therefore that she help me.

And Jesus answered and said unto her, Martha, Martha, thou art careful and troubled about many things:

But one thing is needful: and Mary hath chosen that good part, which shall not be taken away from her.

Luke 10:40-42

42

When You Feel Unusual Stress

And He arose, and rebuked the wind, and said unto the sea, Peace, be still. And the wind ceased, and there was a great calm. *Mark 4:39*

And as they thus spake, Jesus Himself stood in the midst of them, and saith unto them, Peace be unto you. *Luke 24:36*

The thief cometh not, but for to steal, and to kill, and to destroy: I am come that they might have life, and that they might have it more abundantly. *John 10:10*

Peace I leave with you, My peace I

give unto you: not as the world giveth, give I unto you. Let not your heart be troubled, neither let it be afraid.

John 14:27

These things I have spoken unto you, that in Me ye might have peace. In the world ye shall have tribulation: but be of good cheer; I have overcome the world. *John 16:33*

And the God of peace shall bruise satan under your feet shortly. The grace of our Lord Jesus Christ be with you. Amen. *Romans 16:20*

Grace be unto you, and peace, from God our Father, and from the Lord Jesus Christ. *1 Corinthians 1:3*

Now we have received, not the spirit of the world, but the Spirit which is of God; that we might know the things that are freely given to us of God. *1 Corinthians 2:12*

Finally, brethren, farewell. Be perfect, be of good comfort, be of one mind, live in peace; and the God of love and peace shall be with you.

2 Corinthians 13:11

That He would grant you, according to the riches of His glory, to be strengthened with might by His Spirit in the inner man;

And to know the love of Christ, which passeth knowledge, that ye might be filled with all the fulness of God. *Ephesians 3:16,19*

And the very God of peace sanctify you wholly; and I pray God your whole spirit and soul and body be preserved blameless unto the coming of our Lord Jesus Christ. *1 Thessalonians 5:23*

Now the Lord of peace Himself give you peace always by all means. The Lord be with you all.

2 Thessalonians 3:16

Notwithstanding the Lord stood with me, and strengthened me; that by me the preaching might be fully known, and that all the Gentiles might hear: and I was delivered out of the mouth of the lion. *2 Timothy 4:17*

Now the God of peace, that brought again from the dead our Lord Jesus, that great shepherd of the sheep, through the blood of the everlasting covenant,

Make you perfect in every good work to do His will, working in you that which is well-pleasing in His sight, through Jesus Christ; to Whom be glory for ever and ever. Amen.

Hebrews 13:20,21

Elias was a man subject to like passions as we are, and he prayed earnestly that it might not rain: and it rained not on the earth by the space of three years and six months.

And he prayed again, and the heaven gave rain, and the earth brought forth her fruit. *James 5:17,18*

Jude, the servant of Jesus Christ, and brother of James, to them that are sanctified by God the Father, and preserved in Jesus Christ, and called:

Jude 1:1

43

When Your Efforts Seem Unappreciated By Others

But the Lord was with Joseph, and shewed him mercy, and gave him favour in the sight of the keeper of the prison.

Genesis 39:21

The Lord bless thee, and keep thee:

The Lord make His face shine upon thee, and be gracious unto thee:

Numbers 6:24,25

Let them curse, but bless thou: when they arise, let them be ashamed; but let thy servant rejoice.

Psalm 109:28

Let not mercy and truth forsake thee: bind them about thy neck; write them upon the table of thine heart:

So shalt thou find favour and good understanding in the sight of God and man. *Proverbs 3:3,4*

Blessed is the man that heareth Me, watching daily at My gates, waiting at the posts of My doors.

For whoso findeth Me findeth life, and shall obtain favour of the Lord.

Proverbs 8:34,35

He that diligently seeketh good procureth favour: but he that seeketh mischief, it shall come unto him.

Proverbs 11:27

When a man's ways please the Lord, he maketh even his enemies to be at peace with him. *Proverbs 16:7*

And Jesus increased in wisdom and stature, and in favour with God and man. *Luke 2:52*

But the Comforter, which is the Holy Ghost, Whom the Father will send in My name, He shall teach you all things, and bring all things to your remembrance, whatsoever I have said unto you. *John 14:26*

Likewise the Spirit also helpeth our infirmities: for we know not what we should pray for as we ought: but the Spirit itself maketh intercession for us with groanings which cannot be uttered. *Romans 8:26*

For the kingdom of God is not meat and drink; but righteousness, and peace, and joy in the Holy Ghost.

For he that in these things serveth Christ is acceptable to God, and approved of men. *Romans 14:17,18*

Let us therefore come boldly unto the throne of grace, that we may obtain mercy, and find grace to help in time of need. *Hebrews 4:16*

44

WHEN YOU FEEL LIKE A FAILURE

Seek the Lord and His strength, seek His face continually.

1 Chronicles 16:11

The righteous also shall hold on His way, and he that hath clean hands shall be stronger and stronger.

Job 17:9

Though he fall, he shall not be utterly cast down: for the Lord upholdeth him with His hand.

Psalm 37:24

The Lord will perfect that which concerneth me: Thy mercy, O Lord, endureth for ever: forsake not the works of Thine own hands.

Psalm 138:8

But the path of the just is as the shining light, that shineth more and more unto the perfect day.

Proverbs 4:18

Therefore turn thou to thy God: keep mercy and judgment, and wait on thy God continually. *Hosea 12:6*

Watch ye, stand fast in the faith, quit you like men, be strong.

1 Corinthians 16:13

And let us not be weary in well-doing: for in due season we shall reap, if we faint not. *Galatians 6:9*

Wherefore take unto you the whole armour of God, that ye may be able to withstand in the evil day, and having done all, to stand.

Praying always with all prayer and supplication in the Spirit, and watching thereunto with all perseverance and supplication for all saints;

Ephesians 6:13,18

Being confident of this very thing, that He which hath begun a good work in you will perform it until the day of Jesus Christ: *Philippians 1:6*

Therefore, my brethren dearly beloved and longed for, my joy and crown, so stand fast in the Lord, my dearly beloved. *Philippians 4:1*

Looking unto Jesus the author and finisher of our faith; Who for the joy that was set before Him endured the cross, despising the shame, and is set down at the right hand of the throne of God. *Hebrews 12:2*

Casting all your care upon Him; for He careth for you.

Be sober, be vigilant; because your adversary the devil, as a roaring lion, walketh about, seeking whom he may devour: *1 Peter 5:7,8*

45

When Others Have Unrealistic Expectations Of You

For wrath killeth the foolish man, and envy slayeth the silly one. *Job 5:2*

My lips shall not speak wickedness, nor my tongue utter deceit. *Job 27:4*

Cease from anger, and forsake wrath: fret not thyself in any wise to do evil. *Psalm 37:8*

He that keepeth his mouth keepeth his life: but he that openeth wide his lips shall have destruction. *Proverbs 13:3*

He that is slow to wrath is of great understanding: but he that is hasty of spirit exalteth folly. *Proverbs 14:29*

A soft answer turneth away wrath: but grievous words stir up anger.
Proverbs 15:1

The discretion of a man deferreth his anger; and it is his glory to pass over a transgression.

A man of great wrath shall suffer punishment: for if Thou deliver him, yet Thou must do it again.
Proverbs 19:11,19

He that hath no rule over his own spirit is like a city that is broken down, and without walls. *Proverbs 25:28*

Seest thou a man that is hasty in his words? there is more hope of a fool than of him. *Proverbs 29:20*

Be not hasty in thy spirit to be angry: for anger resteth in the bosom of fools. *Ecclesiastes 7:9*

But I say unto you, That every idle word that men shall speak, they shall give account thereof in the day of judgment.

For by thy words thou shalt be justified, and by thy words thou shalt be condemned. *Matthew 12:36,37*

Be ye angry, and sin not: let not the sun go down upon your wrath:

Ephesians 4:26

But now ye also put off all these; anger, wrath, malice, blasphemy, filthy communication out of your mouth.

Colossians 3:8

I will therefore that men pray every where, lifting up holy hands, without wrath and doubting.

1 Timothy 2:8

Wherefore, my beloved brethren, let every man be swift to hear, slow to speak, slow to wrath:

For the wrath of man worketh not the righteousness of God.

James 1:19,20

Not rendering evil for evil, or railing for railing: but contrariwise blessing; knowing that ye are thereunto called, that ye should inherit a blessing.

For he that will love life, and see good days, let him refrain his tongue from evil, and his lips that they speak no guile: *1 Peter 3:9,10*

46

When Your Job Is Unfulfilling

For there is hope of a tree, if it be cut down, that it will sprout again, and that the tender branch thereof will not cease. *Job 14:7*

I have set the Lord always before me: because He is at my right hand, I shall not be moved.

Therefore my heart is glad, and my glory rejoiceth: my flesh also shall rest in hope. *Psalm 16:8,9*

And I will restore to you the years that the locust hath eaten, the cankerworm, and the caterpiller, and the palmerworm, my great army which I sent among you. *Joel 2:25*

I am the vine, ye are the branches: He that abideth in Me, and I in him, the same bringeth forth much fruit: for without Me ye can do nothing.

Herein is My Father glorified, that ye bear much fruit; so shall ye be My disciples. *John 15:5,8*

And be not conformed to this world: but be ye transformed by the renewing of your mind, that ye may prove what is that good, and acceptable, and perfect, will of God.

Rejoicing in hope; patient in tribulation; continuing instant in prayer; *Romans 12:2,12*

For which cause we faint not; but though our outward man perish, yet the inward man is renewed day by day.

While we look not at the things which are seen, but at the things which are not seen: for the things which are seen are temporal; but the things which are not seen are eternal.

2 Corinthians 4:16,18

And be renewed in the spirit of your mind; *Ephesians 4:23*

Brethren, I count not myself to have apprehended: but this one thing I do, forgetting those things which are behind, and reaching forth unto those things which are before,

I press toward the mark for the prize of the high calling of God in Christ Jesus. *Philippians 3:13,14*

47

WHEN YOU MAKE A MAJOR CAREER DECISION

And the Lord, He it is that doth go before thee; He will be with thee, He will not fail thee, neither forsake thee: fear not, neither be dismayed.

Deuteronomy 31:8

Have not I commanded thee? Be strong and of a good courage; be not afraid, neither be thou dismayed: for the Lord thy God is with thee whithersoever thou goest. *Joshua 1:9*

Be ye strong therefore, and let not your hands be weak: for your work shall be rewarded. *2 Chronicles 15:7*

For the eyes of the Lord run to and fro throughout the whole earth, to shew

Himself strong in the behalf of them whose heart is perfect toward Him. Herein thou hast done foolishly: therefore from henceforth thou shalt have wars. *2 Chronicles 16:9*

And they rose early in the morning, and went forth into the wilderness of Tekoa: and as they went forth, Jehoshaphat stood and said, Hear me, O Judah, and ye inhabitants of Jerusalem; Believe in the Lord your God, so shall ye be established; believe His prophets, so shall ye prosper.
2 Chronicles 20:20

Offer the sacrifices of righteousness, and put your trust in the Lord.
Psalm 4:5

For the Lord shall be thy confidence, and shall keep thy foot from being taken. *Proverbs 3:26*

Righteous lips are the delight of kings; and they love Him that speaketh right. *Proverbs 16:13*

Thou wilt keep him in perfect peace, whose mind is stayed on Thee: because he trusteth in Thee.

Isaiah 26:3

Fear thou not; for I am with thee: be not dismayed; for I am thy God: I will strengthen thee; yea, I will help thee; yea, I will uphold thee with the right hand of My righteousness.

Isaiah 41:10

I have declared, and have saved, and I have shewed, when there was no strange god among you: therefore ye are My witnesses, saith the Lord, that I am God. *Isaiah 43:12*

The Lord thy God in the midst of thee is mighty; He will save, He will rejoice over thee with joy; He will rest in His love, He will joy over thee with singing. *Zephaniah 3:17*

He staggered not at the promise of God through unbelief; but was strong in faith, giving glory to God;

And being fully persuaded that, what He had promised, He was able also to perform. *Romans 4:20,21*

For to one is given by the Spirit the word of wisdom; to another the word of knowledge by the same Spirit;

To another faith by the same Spirit; to another the gifts of healing by the same Spirit; *1 Corinthians 12:8,9*

But my God shall supply all your need according to His riches in glory by Christ Jesus. *Philippians 4:19*

If any of you lack wisdom, let him ask of God, that giveth to all men liberally, and upbraideth not; and it shall be given him. *James 1:5*

Greet ye one another with a kiss of charity. Peace be with you all that are in Christ Jesus. Amen. *1 Peter 5:14*

48

WHEN YOU GET FIRED FROM YOUR JOB

The steps of a good man are ordered by the Lord: and He delighteth in his way.

Though he fall, he shall not be utterly cast down: for the Lord upholdeth him with His hand.

Psalm 37:23,24

Why art thou cast down, O my soul? and why art thou disquieted in me? hope thou in God: for I shall yet praise Him for the help of His countenance. *Psalm 42:5*

And call upon Me in the day of trouble: I will deliver thee, and thou shalt glorify Me. *Psalm 50:15*

Cast thy burden upon the Lord, and He shall sustain thee: He shall never suffer the righteous to be moved.

Psalm 55:22

Though I walk in the midst of trouble, Thou wilt revive me: Thou shalt stretch forth Thine hand against the wrath of mine enemies, and Thy right hand shall save me.

The Lord will perfect that which concerneth me: Thy mercy, O Lord, endureth for ever: forsake not the works of Thine own hands.

Psalm 138:7,8

I returned, and saw under the sun, that the race is not to the swift, nor the battle to the strong, neither yet bread to the wise, nor yet riches to men of understanding, nor yet favour to men of skill; but time and chance happeneth to them all. *Ecclesiastes 9:11*

Blessed are they that mourn: for they shall be comforted. *Matthew 5:4*

Are not two sparrows sold for a farthing? and one of them shall not fall on the ground without your Father.

But the very hairs of your head are all numbered.

Fear ye not therefore, ye are of more value than many sparrows.

Matthew 10:29-31

And we know that all things work together for good to them that love God, to them who are the called according to His purpose. *Romans 8:28*

There hath no temptation taken you but such as is common to man: but God is faithful, Who will not suffer you to be tempted above that ye are able; but will with the temptation also make a way to escape, that ye may be able to bear it. *1 Corinthians 10:13*

We are troubled on every side, yet not distressed; we are perplexed, but not in despair;

Persecuted, but not forsaken; cast down, but not destroyed;

2 Corinthians 4:8,9

Put on the whole armour of God, that ye may be able to stand against the wiles of the devil.

For we wrestle not against flesh and blood, but against principalities, against powers, against the rulers of the darkness of this world, against spiritual wickedness in high places.

Wherefore take unto you the whole armour of God, that ye may be able to withstand in the evil day, and having done all, to stand.

Stand therefore, having your loins girt about with truth, and having on the breastplate of righteousness;

Above all, taking the shield of faith, wherewith ye shall be able to quench all the fiery darts of the wicked.

Ephesians 6:11-14,16

For we have not an high priest which cannot be touched with the feeling of our infirmities; but was in all points tempted like as we are, yet without sin.

Let us therefore come boldly unto the throne of grace, that we may obtain mercy, and find grace to help in time of need. *Hebrews 4:15,16*

YOUR DAILY SCHEDULE

49

WHEN YOU HAVE OVERBOOKED YOUR SCHEDULE

He maketh me to lie down in green pastures: He leadeth me beside the still waters.

He restoreth my soul: He leadeth me in the paths of righteousness for His name's sake. *Psalm 23:2,3*

Shew me Thy ways, O Lord; teach me Thy paths.

Lead me in Thy truth, and teach me: for Thou art the God of my salvation; on Thee do I wait all the day.

Let integrity and uprightness preserve me; for I wait on Thee.

Psalm 25:4,5,21

Wait on the Lord: be of good courage, and He shall strengthen thine heart: wait, I say, on the Lord.

Psalm 27:14

But they that wait upon the Lord shall renew their strength; they shall mount up with wings as eagles; they shall run, and not be weary; and they shall walk, and not faint. *Isaiah 40:31*

For what is a man profited, if he shall gain the whole world, and lose his own soul? or what shall a man give in exchange for his soul? *Matthew 16:26*

And He said unto them, Come ye yourselves apart into a desert place, and rest a while: for there were many coming and going, and they had no leisure so much as to eat. *Mark 6:31*

And take heed to yourselves, lest at any time your hearts be overcharged with surfeiting, and drunkenness, and cares of this life, and so that day come upon you unawares. *Luke 21:34*

But if any provide not for his own, and specially for those of his own house, he hath denied the faith, and is worse than an infidel. *1 Timothy 5:8*

Keep yourselves in the love of God, looking for the mercy of our Lord Jesus Christ unto eternal life. *Jude 1:21*

50

When You Feel Disorganized

The Lord is my shepherd; I shall not want. *Psalm 23:1*

Shew me Thy ways, O Lord; teach me Thy paths. *Psalm 25:4*

O fear the Lord, ye His saints: for there is no want to them that fear Him.

The young lions do lack, and suffer hunger: but they that seek the Lord shall not want any good thing.

Psalm 34:9,10

My confusion is continually before me, and the shame of my face hath covered me, *Psalm 44:15*

Behold, as the eyes of servants look unto the hand of their masters, and as the eyes of a maiden unto the hand of her mistress; so our eyes wait upon the Lord our God, until that He have mercy upon us. *Psalm 123:2*

For the Lord shall be thy confidence, and shall keep thy foot from being taken. *Proverbs 3:26*

Keep thy heart with all diligence; for out of it are the issues of life. *Proverbs 4:23*

Go to the ant, thou sluggard; consider her ways, and be wise:

Which having no guide, overseer, or ruler,

Provideth her meat in the summer, and gathereth her food in the harvest.

How long wilt thou sleep, O sluggard? when wilt thou arise out of thy sleep? *Proverbs 6:6-9*

And we have sent with them our brother, whom we have oftentimes proved diligent in many things, but now much more diligent, upon the great confidence which I have in you. *2 Corinthians 8:22*

51

When You Become Frustrated By Unnecessary Interruptions

God is my strength and power: And He maketh my way perfect.

He maketh my feet like hinds' feet: and setteth me upon my high places.

For Thou hast girded me with strength to battle: them that rose up against me hast Thou subdued under me. *2 Samuel 22:33,34,40*

Seek the Lord and His strength, seek His face continually.

1 Chronicles 16:11

Then He said unto them, Go your way, eat the fat, and drink the sweet, and send portions unto them for whom nothing is prepared: for this day is holy unto our Lord: neither be ye sorry; for the joy of the Lord is your strength.

Nehemiah 8:10

Better is the end of a thing than the beginning thereof: and the patient in spirit is better than the proud in spirit.

Be not hasty in thy spirit to be angry: for anger resteth in the bosom of fools. *Ecclesiastes 7:8,9*

Blessed are the merciful: for they shall obtain mercy.

Give to him that asketh thee, and from him that would borrow of thee turn not thou away. *Matthew 5:7,42*

Take My yoke upon you, and learn of Me; for I am meek and lowly in heart: and ye shall find rest unto your souls.

Matthew 11:29

If it be possible, as much as lieth in you, live peaceably with all men.

Romans 12:18

Charity suffereth long, and is kind; charity envieth not; charity vaunteth not itself, is not puffed up,

1 Corinthians 13:4

52

WHEN WORK ROBS YOU OF IMPORTANT FAMILY TIME

For I know Him, that He will command His children and His household after Him, and they shall keep the way of the Lord, to do justice and judgment; that the Lord may bring upon Abraham that which He hath spoken of him. *Genesis 18:19*

Only take heed to thyself, and keep thy soul diligently, lest thou forget the things which thine eyes have seen, and lest they depart from thy heart all the days of thy life: but teach them thy sons, and thy sons' sons;

Deuteronomy 4:9

And these words, which I command thee this day, shall be in thine heart:

And thou shalt teach them diligently unto thy children, and shalt talk of them when thou sittest in thine house, and when thou walkest by the way, and when thou liest down, and when thou risest up.

Deuteronomy 6:6,7

But seek ye first the kingdom of God, and His righteousness; and all these things shall be added unto you.

Matthew 6:33

If a son shall ask bread of any of you that is a father, will he give him a stone? or if he ask a fish, will he for a fish give him a serpent?

Or if he shall ask an egg, will he offer him a scorpion? *Luke 11:11,12*

For the promise is unto you, and to your children, and to all that are afar off, even as many as the Lord our God shall call. *Acts 2:39*

And they said, Believe on the Lord Jesus Christ, and thou shalt be saved, and thy house. *Acts 16:31*

And, ye fathers, provoke not your children to wrath: but bring them up in the nurture and admonition of the Lord. *Ephesians 6:4*

Fathers, provoke not your children to anger, lest they be discouraged. *Colossians 3:21*

Let the deacons be the husbands of one wife, ruling their children and their own houses well. *1 Timothy 3:12*

But if any provide not for his own, and specially for those of his own house, he hath denied the faith, and is worse than an infidel. *1 Timothy 5:8*

53

WHEN YOU NEED TIME AWAY FROM THE DEMANDS OF OTHERS

In my distress I called upon the Lord, and cried to my God: and He did hear my voice out of His temple, and my cry did enter into His ears.

God is my strength and power: And He maketh my way perfect.

For Thou hast girded me with strength to battle: them that rose up against me hast Thou subdued under me. *2 Samuel 22:7,33,40*

Thou, O God, didst send a plentiful rain, whereby Thou didst confirm Thine inheritance, when it was weary.

Psalm 68:9

I called upon the Lord in distress: the Lord answered me, and set me in a large place. *Psalm 118:5*

In my distress I cried unto the Lord, and He heard me. *Psalm 120:1*

For thou hast been a strength to the poor, a strength to the needy in his distress, a refuge from the storm, a shadow from the heat, when the blast of the terrible ones is as a storm against the wall. *Isaiah 25:4*

He giveth power to the faint; and to them that have no might He increaseth strength.

Even the youths shall faint and be weary, and the young men shall utterly fall:

But they that wait upon the Lord shall renew their strength; they shall mount up with wings as eagles; they shall run, and not be weary; and they shall walk, and not faint.

Isaiah 40:29-31

The Lord God hath given me the tongue of the learned, that I should know how to speak a word in season to him that is weary: He wakeneth morning by morning, He wakeneth mine ear to hear as the learned.

Isaiah 50:4

Thou art wearied in the greatness of thy way; yet saidst thou not, There is no hope: thou hast found the life of thine hand; therefore thou wast not grieved. *Isaiah 57:10*

If thou hast run with the footmen, and they have wearied thee, then how canst thou contend with horses? and if in the land of peace, wherein thou trustedst, they wearied thee, then how wilt thou do in the swelling of Jordan?

Jeremiah 12:5

And there appeared an angel unto him from heaven, strengthening him.

Luke 22:43

I can do all things through Christ

which strengtheneth me.

Philippians 4:13

But ye, brethren, be not weary in well-doing. *2 Thessalonians 3:13*

Quenched the violence of fire, escaped the edge of the sword, out of weakness were made strong, waxed valiant in fight, turned to flight the armies of the aliens. *Hebrews 11:34*

54

WHEN DAILY FAMILY DEVOTIONS SEEM DIFFICULT

For I know him, that he will command his children and his household after him, and they shall keep the way of the Lord, to do justice and judgment; that the Lord may bring upon Abraham that which He hath spoken of him. *Genesis 18:19*

Only take heed to thyself, and keep thy soul diligently, lest thou forget the things which thine eyes have seen, and lest they depart from thy heart all the days of thy life: but teach them thy sons, and thy sons' sons;

Deuteronomy 4:9

And these words, which I command thee this day, shall be in thine heart:

And thou shalt teach them diligently unto thy children, and shalt talk of them when thou sittest in thine house, and when thou walkest by the way, and when thou liest down, and when thou risest up. *Deuteronomy 6:6,7*

And ye shall teach them your children, speaking of them when thou sittest in thine house, and when thou walkest by the way, when thou liest down, and when thou risest up.

Deuteronomy 11:19

And if it seem evil unto you to serve the Lord, choose you this day whom ye will serve; whether the gods which your fathers served that were on the other side of the flood, or the gods of the Amorites, in whose land ye dwell: but as for me and my house, we will serve the Lord. *Joshua 24:15*

I will open my mouth in a parable:

I will utter dark sayings of old:
Which we have heard and known, and our fathers have told us.
Psalm 78:2,3

A good man leaveth an inheritance to his children's children: and the wealth of the sinner is laid up for the just. *Proverbs 13:22*

He that is greedy of gain troubleth his own house; but he that hateth gifts shall live. *Proverbs 15:27*

Better is a dry morsel, and quietness therewith, than an house full of sacrifices with strife. *Proverbs 17:1*

The just man walketh in his integrity: his children are blessed after him. *Proverbs 20:7*

Train up a child in the way he should go: and when he is old, he will not depart from it. *Proverbs 22:6*

Through wisdom is an house

builded; and by understanding it is established: *Proverbs 24:3*

Correct thy son, and he shall give thee rest; yea, he shall give delight unto thy soul. *Proverbs 29:17*

Your Finances

55

When Your Job Security Is Threatened

While the earth remaineth, seedtime and harvest, and cold and heat, and summer and winter, and day and night shall not cease. *Genesis 8:22*

For there is hope of a tree, if it be cut down, that it will sprout again, and that the tender branch thereof will not cease.

Though the root thereof wax old in the earth, and the stock thereof die in the ground;

Yet through the scent of water it will bud, and bring forth boughs like a plant. *Job 14:7-9*

I have set the Lord always before me: because He is at my right hand, I shall not be moved. *Psalm 16:8*

And in my prosperity I said, I shall never be moved. *Psalm 30:6*

Cast thy burden upon the Lord, and He shall sustain thee: He shall never suffer the righteous to be moved. *Psalm 55:22*

They that trust in the Lord shall be as mount Zion, which cannot be removed, but abideth for ever. *Psalm 125:1*

For the mountains shall depart, and the hills be removed; but My kindness shall not depart from thee, neither shall the covenant of My peace be removed, saith the Lord that hath mercy on thee. *Isaiah 54:10*

He hath also broken my teeth with gravel stones, He hath covered me with ashes.

And Thou hast removed my soul far off from peace: I forgat prosperity.

And I said, My strength and my hope is perished from the Lord:

Remembering mine affliction and my misery, the wormwood and the gall.

Lamentations 3:16-19

For I am the Lord, I change not; therefore ye sons of Jacob are not consumed. *Malachi 3:6*

Jesus Christ the same yesterday, and to-day, and for ever. *Hebrews 13:8*

Every good gift and every perfect gift is from above, and cometh down from the Father of lights, with Whom is no variableness, neither shadow of turning. *James 1:17*

56

WHEN YOU FACE BANKRUPTCY

The Lord bless thee, and keep thee:

The Lord make His face shine upon thee, and be gracious unto thee:

The Lord lift up His countenance upon thee, and give thee peace.

Numbers 6:24-26

For the Lord thy God is a merciful God; He will not forsake thee, neither destroy thee, nor forget the covenant of thy fathers which He sware unto them.

Deuteronomy 4:31

Be strong and of a good courage, fear not, nor be afraid of them: for the Lord thy God, He it is that doth go with thee; He will not fail thee, nor forsake thee.

And the Lord, He it is that doth go before thee; He will be with thee, He will not fail thee, neither forsake thee: fear not, neither be dismayed.

Deuteronomy 31:6,8

I had fainted, unless I had believed to see the goodness of the Lord in the land of the living.

Wait on the Lord: be of good courage, and He shall strengthen thine heart: wait, I say, on the Lord.

Psalm 27:13,14

My times are in Thy hand: deliver me from the hand of mine enemies, and from them that persecute me.

Make Thy face to shine upon Thy servant: save me for Thy mercies' sake.

Psalm 31:15,16

I know both how to be abased, and I know how to abound: every where and in all things I am instructed both to be full and to be hungry, both to abound and to suffer need.

I can do all things through Christ which strengtheneth me.

Notwithstanding ye have well done, that ye did communicate with my affliction. *Philippians 4:12-14*

But my God shall supply all your need according to His riches in glory by Christ Jesus. *Philippians 4:19*

Let your conversation be without covetousness; and be content with such things as ye have: for He hath said, I will never leave thee, nor forsake thee.

So that we may boldly say, The Lord is my helper, and I will not fear what man shall do unto me.

Hebrews 13:5,6

Behold, we count them happy which endure. Ye have heard of the patience of Job, and have seen the end of the Lord; that the Lord is very pitiful, and of tender mercy.

Is any among you afflicted? let him pray. Is any merry? let him sing psalms.

Confess your faults one to another, and pray one for another, that ye may be healed. The effectual fervent prayer of a righteous man availeth much.

James 5:11,13,16

Wherein ye greatly rejoice, though now for a season, if need be, ye are in heaviness through manifold temptations:

That the trial of your faith, being much more precious than of gold that perisheth, though it be tried with fire, might be found unto praise and honour and glory at the appearing of Jesus Christ: *1 Peter 1:6,7*

Casting all your care upon Him; for He careth for you. *1 Peter 5:7*

57

WHEN YOU NEED CREATIVE IDEAS FOR FINANCIAL FREEDOM

Now therefore go, and I will be with thy mouth, and teach thee what thou shalt say. *Exodus 4:12*

But there is a spirit in man: and the inspiration of the Almighty giveth them understanding. *Job 32:8*

Then He openeth the ears of men, and sealeth their instruction,

Job 33:16

I will bless the Lord, Who hath given me counsel: my reins also instruct me in the night seasons.

Psalm 16:7

I will instruct thee and teach thee in the way which thou shalt go: I will guide thee with Mine eye. *Psalm 32:8*

For with thee is the fountain of life: in thy light shall we see light.
Psalm 36:9

I wisdom dwell with prudence, and find out knowledge of witty inventions.
I love them that love Me; and those that seek Me early shall find Me.
Riches and honour are with Me; yea, durable riches and righteousness.
That I may cause those that love Me to inherit substance; and I will fill their treasures.
For whoso findeth Me findeth life, and shall obtain favour of the Lord.
Proverbs 8:12,17,18,21,35

Whoso is simple, let him turn in hither: as for him that wanteth understanding, she saith to him,
Come, eat of my bread, and drink of the wine which I have mingled.
Proverbs 9:4,5

For by Me thy days shall be multiplied, and the years of thy life shall be increased.

If thou be wise, thou shalt be wise for thyself: but if thou scornest, thou alone shalt bear it. *Proverbs 9:11,12*

He that handleth a matter wisely shall find good: and whoso trusteth in the Lord, happy is he.

The wise in heart shall be called prudent: and the sweetness of the lips increaseth learning.

Understanding is a wellspring of life unto him that hath it: but the instruction of fools is folly.

The heart of the wise teacheth his mouth, and addeth learning to his lips.

Pleasant words are as an honeycomb, sweet to the soul, and health to the bones. *Proverbs 16:20-24*

The heart of the prudent getteth knowledge; and the ear of the wise seeketh knowledge. *Proverbs 18:15*

My son, eat thou honey, because it

is good; and the honeycomb, which is sweet to thy taste:

So shall the knowledge of wisdom be unto thy soul: when thou hast found it, then there shall be a reward, and thy expectation shall not be cut off.

Proverbs 24:13,14

Evil men understand not judgment: but they that seek the Lord understand all things. *Proverbs 28:5*

Who is as the wise man? and who knoweth the interpretation of a thing? a man's wisdom maketh his face to shine, and the boldness of his face shall be changed.

Whoso keepeth the commandment shall feel no evil thing: and a wise man's heart discerneth both time and judgment. *Ecclesiastes 8:1,5*

The words of the wise are as goads, and as nails fastened by the masters of assemblies, which are given from one shepherd. *Ecclesiastes 12:11*

And wisdom and knowledge shall be the stability of thy times, and strength of salvation: the fear of the Lord is his treasure. *Isaiah 33:6*

The light of the body is the eye: if therefore thine eye be single, thy whole body shall be full of light.

But if thine eye be evil, thy whole body shall be full of darkness. If therefore the light that is in thee be darkness, how great is that darkness!

Matthew 6:22,23

And ye shall know the truth, and the truth shall make you free.

John 8:32

58

When You Have Spent Money Unwisely

And the Lord appeared unto him the same night, and said, I am the God of Abraham thy father: fear not, for I am with thee, and will bless thee, and multiply thy seed for My servant Abraham's sake. *Genesis 26:24*

Behold, the Lord thy God hath set the land before thee: go up and possess it, as the Lord God of thy fathers hath said unto thee; fear not, neither be discouraged. *Deuteronomy 1:21*

It is better to trust in the Lord than to put confidence in man.
Psalm 118:8

Strengthen ye the weak hands, and confirm the feeble knees.

Say to them that are of a fearful heart, Be strong, fear not: behold, your God will come with vengeance, even God with a recompence; He will come and save you. *Isaiah 35:3,4*

Fear thou not; for I am with thee: be not dismayed; for I am thy God: I will strengthen thee; yea, I will help thee; yea, I will uphold thee with the right hand of My righteousness.

Isaiah 41:10

He delivereth and rescueth, and He worketh signs and wonders in heaven and in earth, Who hath delivered Daniel from the power of the lions. *Daniel 6:27*

Take therefore no thought for the morrow: for the morrow shall take thought for the things of itself. Sufficient unto the day is the evil thereof. *Matthew 6:34*

Not that we are sufficient of ourselves to think any thing as of ourselves; but our sufficiency is of God;

2 Corinthians 3:5

And God is able to make all grace abound toward you; that ye, always having all sufficiency in all things, may abound to every good work:

2 Corinthians 9:8

And He said unto me, My grace is sufficient for thee: for My strength is made perfect in weakness. Most gladly therefore will I rather glory in my infirmities, that the power of Christ may rest upon me. *2 Corinthians 12:9*

Be careful for nothing; but in every thing by prayer and supplication with thanksgiving let your requests be made known unto God.

Not that I speak in respect of want: for I have learned, in whatsoever state I am, therewith to be content.

Philippians 4:6,11

I know both how to be abased, and I know how to abound: every where and in all things I am instructed both to be full and to be hungry, both to abound and to suffer need.

I can do all things through Christ which strengtheneth me.

But my God shall supply all your need according to His riches in glory by Christ Jesus. *Philippians 4:12,13,19*

For we have not an high priest which cannot be touched with the feeling of our infirmities; but was in all points tempted like as we are, yet without sin.

Let us therefore come boldly unto the throne of grace, that we may obtain mercy, and find grace to help in time of need. *Hebrews 4:15,16*

59

WHEN YOU NEED WISDOM ABOUT BORROWING MONEY

The steps of a good man are ordered by the Lord: and He delighteth in his way. *Psalm 37:23*

For I the Lord thy God will hold thy right hand, saying unto thee, Fear not; I will help thee.

Fear not, thou worm Jacob, and ye men of Israel; I will help thee, saith the Lord, and thy redeemer, the Holy One of Israel.

When the poor and needy seek water, and there is none, and their tongue faileth for thirst, I the Lord will hear them, I the God of Israel will not forsake them. *Isaiah 41:13,14,17*

Although the fig tree shall not blossom, neither shall fruit be in the vines; the labour of the olive shall fail, and the fields shall yield no meat; the flock shall be cut off from the fold, and there shall be no herd in the stalls:

Yet I will rejoice in the Lord, I will joy in the God of my salvation.

Habakkuk 3:17,18

Therefore I say unto you, Take no thought for your life, what ye shall eat, or what ye shall drink; nor yet for your body, what ye shall put on. Is not the life more than meat, and the body than raiment?

Wherefore, if God so clothe the grass of the field, which to-day is, and to-morrow is cast into the oven, shall He not much more clothe you, O ye of little faith?

But seek ye first the kingdom of God, and His righteousness; and all these things shall be added unto you.

Take therefore no thought for the morrow: for the morrow shall take thought for the things of itself.

Sufficient unto the day is the evil thereof. *Matthew 6:25,30,33,34*

Blessed are ye that hunger now: for ye shall be filled. Blessed are ye that weep now: for ye shall laugh.
Luke 6:21

And we know that all things work together for good to them that love God, to them who are the called according to His purpose. *Romans 8:28*

I can do all things through Christ which strengtheneth me.

But my God shall supply all your need according to His riches in glory by Christ Jesus. *Philippians 4:13,19*

Wherein ye greatly rejoice, though now for a season, if need be, ye are in heaviness through manifold temptations:

That the trial of your faith, being much more precious than of gold that perisheth, though it be tried with fire, might be found unto praise and honour and glory at the appearing of Jesus

Christ: *1 Peter 1:6,7*

Casting all your care upon Him; for He careth for you. *1 Peter 5:7*

60

WHEN TITHING TO THE WORK OF GOD SEEMS DIFFICULT

The gold for things of gold, and the silver for things of silver, and for all manner of work to be made by the hands of artificers. And who then is willing to consecrate his service this day unto the Lord? *1 Chronicles 29:5*

Be ye strong therefore, and let not your hands be weak: for your work shall be rewarded. *2 Chronicles 15:7*

Vow, and pay unto the Lord your God: let all that be round about Him bring presents unto Him that ought to be feared. *Psalm 76:11*

A good man sheweth favour, and lendeth: he will guide his affairs with discretion.

He hath dispersed, he hath given to the poor; his righteousness endureth for ever; his horn shall be exalted with honour. *Psalm 112:5,9*

Honour the Lord with thy substance, and with the firstfruits of all thine increase:

So shall thy barns be filled with plenty, and thy presses shall burst out with new wine. *Proverbs 3:9,10*

There is that scattereth, and yet increaseth; and there is that withholdeth more than is meet, but it tendeth to poverty.

The liberal soul shall be made fat: and he that watereth shall be watered also himself. *Proverbs 11:24,25*

There is that maketh himself rich, yet hath nothing: there is that maketh himself poor, yet hath great riches. *Proverbs 13:7*

He that hath pity upon the poor lendeth unto the Lord; and that which he hath given will He pay him again.
Proverbs 19:17

He coveteth greedily all the day long: but the righteous giveth and spareth not. *Proverbs 21:26*

He that hath a bountiful eye shall be blessed; for he giveth of his bread to the poor. *Proverbs 22:9*

He that giveth unto the poor shall not lack: but he that hideth his eyes shall have many a curse.
Proverbs 28:27

Cast thy bread upon the waters: for thou shalt find it after many days.

Give a portion to seven, and also to eight; for thou knowest not what evil shall be upon the earth.
Ecclesiastes 11:1,2

But the liberal deviseth liberal things; and by liberal things shall he stand. *Isaiah 32:8*

Bring ye all the tithes into the storehouse, that there may be meat in Mine house, and prove Me now herewith, saith the Lord of hosts, if I will not open you the windows of heaven, and pour you out a blessing, that there shall not be room enough to receive it.

And I will rebuke the devourer for your sakes, and he shall not destroy the fruits of your ground; neither shall your vine cast her fruit before the time in the field, saith the Lord of hosts.

Malachi 3:10,11

Give, and it shall be given unto you; good measure, pressed down, and shaken together, and running over, shall men give into your bosom. For with the same measure that ye mete withal it shall be measured to you again. *Luke 6:38*

Or he that exhorteth, on exhortation: he that giveth, let him do it with simplicity; he that ruleth, with diligence; he that sheweth mercy, with cheerfulness. *Romans 12:8*

Upon the first day of the week let every one of you lay by him in store, as God hath prospered him, that there be no gatherings when I come.

1 Corinthians 16:2

But this I say, He which soweth sparingly shall reap also sparingly; and he which soweth bountifully shall reap also bountifully.

Every man according as he purposeth in his heart, so let him give; not grudgingly, or of necessity: for God loveth a cheerful giver.

And God is able to make all grace abound toward you; that ye, always having all sufficiency in all things, may abound to every good work:

2 Corinthians 9:6-8

Charge them that are rich in this world, that they be not highminded, nor trust in uncertain riches, but in the living God, who giveth us richly all things to enjoy;

That they do good, that they be rich in good works, ready to distribute, willing to communicate;

Laying up in store for themselves a good foundation against the time to come, that they may lay hold on eternal life. *1 Timothy 6:17-19*

But whoso hath this world's good, and seeth his brother have need, and shutteth up his bowels of compassion from him, how dwelleth the love of God in him?

My little children, let us not love in word, neither in tongue; but in deed and in truth. *1 John 3:17,18*

61

When Your Children Need To Learn The Blessing Of Work

Thou shalt not oppress an hired servant that is poor and needy, whether he be of thy brethren, or of thy strangers that are in thy land within thy gates:

At his day thou shalt give him his hire, neither shall the sun go down upon it; for he is poor, and setteth his heart upon it: lest he cry against thee unto the Lord, and it be sin unto thee.

Deuteronomy 24:14,15

Thou shalt not muzzle the ox when he treadeth out the corn.

Deuteronomy 25:4

He becometh poor that dealeth

with a slack hand: but the hand of the diligent maketh rich. *Proverbs 10:4*

He that tilleth his land shall be satisfied with bread: but he that followeth vain persons is void of understanding.

The hand of the diligent shall bear rule: but the slothful shall be under tribute.

The slothful man roasteth not that which he took in hunting: but the substance of a diligent man is precious.

Proverbs 12:11,24,27

Wealth gotten by vanity shall be diminished: but he that gathereth by labour shall increase. *Proverbs 13:11*

In all labour there is profit: but the talk of the lips tendeth only to penury. *Proverbs 14:23*

Love not sleep, lest thou come to poverty; open thine eyes, and thou shalt be satisfied with bread.

Proverbs 20:13

Seest thou a man diligent in his business? he shall stand before kings; he shall not stand before mean men.

Proverbs 22:29

He that tilleth his land shall have plenty of bread: but he that followeth after vain persons shall have poverty enough. *Proverbs 28:19*

The sleep of a labouring man is sweet, whether he eat little or much: but the abundance of the rich will not suffer him to sleep. *Ecclesiastes 5:12*

YOUR CHURCH

62

WHEN CHURCH CONFLICTS DISILLUSION YOU

The Lord is my strength and my shield; my heart trusted in Him, and I am helped: therefore my heart greatly rejoiceth; and with my song will I praise Him. *Psalm 28:7*

For I have heard the slander of many: fear was on every side: while they took counsel together against me, they devised to take away my life.

But I trusted in Thee, O Lord: I said, Thou art my God.

My times are in Thy hand: deliver

me from the hand of mine enemies, and from them that persecute me.

Make Thy face to shine upon Thy servant: save me for Thy mercies' sake.

Psalm 31:13-16

The angel of the Lord encampeth round about them that fear Him, and delivereth them. *Psalm 34:7*

Thou lovest evil more than good; and lying rather than to speak righteousness.

Thou lovest all devouring words, O thou deceitful tongue.

God shall likewise destroy thee for ever, He shall take thee away, and pluck thee out of thy dwelling place, and root thee out of the land of the living.

Psalm 52:3-5

In the day of my trouble I will call upon Thee: for Thou wilt answer me.

Psalm 86:7

He shall cover thee with His feathers, and under His wings shalt thou trust: His truth shall be thy shield and buckler.

Thou shalt not be afraid for the terror by night; nor for the arrow that flieth by day; *Psalm 91:4,5*

Buy the truth, and sell it not; also wisdom, and instruction, and understanding. *Proverbs 23:23*

For the Lord God will help me; therefore shall I not be confounded: therefore have I set my face like a flint, and I know that I shall not be ashamed.

He is near that justifieth me; who will contend with me? let us stand together: who is mine adversary? let him come near to me.

Behold, the Lord God will help me; who is he that shall condemn me? lo, they all shall wax old as a garment; the moth shall eat them up. *Isaiah 50:7-9*

Thus saith the Lord; Cursed be the man that trusteth in man, and maketh flesh his arm, and whose heart departeth from the Lord.

For he shall be like the heath in the desert, and shall not see when good cometh; but shall inhabit the parched places in the wilderness, in a salt land and not inhabited.

Blessed is the man that trusteth in the Lord, and whose hope the Lord is.

For he shall be as a tree planted by the waters, and that spreadeth out her roots by the river, and shall not see when heat cometh, but her leaf shall be green; and shall not be careful in the year of drought, neither shall cease from yielding fruit. *Jeremiah 17:5-8*

But I will deliver thee in that day, saith the Lord: and thou shalt not be given into the hand of the men of whom thou art afraid.

For I will surely deliver thee, and thou shalt not fall by the sword, but thy life shall be for a prey unto thee: because thou hast put thy trust in Me, saith the Lord. *Jeremiah 39:17,18*

Rejoice not against me, O mine enemy: when I fall, I shall arise; when

I sit in darkness, the Lord shall be a light unto me. *Micah 7:8*

Wherefore putting away lying, speak every man truth with his neighbour: for we are members one of another.

Be ye angry, and sin not: let not the sun go down upon your wrath:

And grieve not the Holy Spirit of God, whereby ye are sealed unto the day of redemption.

Let all bitterness, and wrath, and anger, and clamour, and evil speaking, be put away from you, with all malice:

Ephesians 4:25,26,30,31

Looking diligently lest any man fail of the grace of God; lest any root of bitterness springing up trouble you, and thereby many be defiled;

Hebrews 12:15

63

When Someone Has Offended You

And the Lord said unto Cain, Why art thou wroth? and why is thy countenance fallen? *Genesis 4:6*

For wrath killeth the foolish man, and envy slayeth the silly one. *Job 5:2*

Be ye afraid of the sword: for wrath bringeth the punishments of the sword, that ye may know there is a judgment. *Job 19:29*

Cease from anger, and forsake wrath: fret not thyself in any wise to do evil. *Psalm 37:8*

For jealousy is the rage of a man: therefore he will not spare in the day of vengeance. *Proverbs 6:34*

A fool's wrath is presently known: but a prudent man covereth shame.
Proverbs 12:16

He that is soon angry dealeth foolishly: and a man of wicked devices is hated.

He that is slow to wrath is of great understanding: but he that is hasty of spirit exalteth folly. *Proverbs 14:17,29*

A soft answer turneth away wrath: but grievous words stir up anger.
Proverbs 15:1

Lest thou learn His ways, and get a snare to thy soul. *Proverbs 22:25*

He that hath no rule over his own spirit is like a city that is broken down, and without walls. *Proverbs 25:28*

Wrath is cruel, and anger is outrageous; but who is able to stand before envy? *Proverbs 27:4*

Be not hasty in thy spirit to be angry: for anger resteth in the bosom of fools. *Ecclesiastes 7:9*

But I say unto you, That whosoever is angry with his brother without a cause shall be in danger of the judgment: and whosoever shall say to his brother, Raca, shall be in danger of the council: but whosoever shall say, Thou fool, shall be in danger of hell fire.
Matthew 5:22

And herein do I exercise myself, to have always a conscience void of offence toward God, and toward men.
Acts 24:16

Give none offence, neither to the Jews, nor to the Gentiles, nor to the church of God: *1 Corinthians 10:32*

Giving no offence in any thing, that the ministry be not blamed:
2 Corinthians 6:3

But now ye also put off all these;

anger, wrath, malice, blasphemy, filthy communication out of your mouth.

Colossians 3:8

Wherefore, my beloved brethren, let every man be swift to hear, slow to speak, slow to wrath:

For the wrath of man worketh not the righteousness of God.

James 1:19,20

Wherefore, beloved, seeing that ye look for such things, be diligent that ye may be found of him in peace, without spot, and blameless. *2 Peter 3:14*

64

When You Are Asked To Accept Special Responsibilities

Behold, as the eyes of servants look unto the hand of their masters, and as the eyes of a maiden unto the hand of her mistress; so our eyes wait upon the Lord our God, until that He have mercy upon us. *Psalm 123:2*

As the cold of snow in the time of harvest, so is a faithful messenger to them that send him: for he refresheth the soul of his masters. *Proverbs 25:13*

Whoso keepeth the fig tree shall eat the fruit thereof: so he that waiteth on his master shall be honoured.
Proverbs 27:18

A son honoureth his father, and a servant his master: if then I be a father, where is Mine honour? and if I be a master, where is My fear? saith the Lord of hosts unto you, O priests, that despise My name. And ye say, Wherein have we despised Thy name?

Malachi 1:6

Even as the Son of man came not to be ministered unto, but to minister, and to give His life a ransom for many.

Matthew 20:28

And when they were come to Him, He said unto them, Ye know, from the first day that I came into Asia, after what manner I have been with you at all seasons,

Serving the Lord with all humility of mind, and with many tears, and temptations, which befell me by the lying in wait of the Jews:

Acts 20:18,19

Moreover it is required in

stewards, that a man be found faithful.
1 Corinthians 4:2

Therefore, my beloved brethren, be ye stedfast, unmoveable, always abounding in the work of the Lord, forasmuch as ye know that your labour is not in vain in the Lord.
1 Corinthians 15:58

With good will doing service, as to the Lord, and not to men:
Ephesians 6:7

So being affectionately desirous of you, we were willing to have imparted unto you, not the gospel of God only, but also our own souls, because ye were dear unto us. *1 Thessalonians 2:8*

65

WHEN YOU FEEL UNQUALIFIED FOR A CHURCH POSITION

And Caleb stilled the people before Moses, and said, Let us go up at once, and possess it; for we are well able to overcome it. *Numbers 13:30*

Give therefore thy servant an understanding heart to judge thy people, that I may discern between good and bad: for who is able to judge this thy so great a people? *1 Kings 3:9*

Be ye strong therefore, and let not your hands be weak: for your work shall be rewarded. *2 Chronicles 15:7*

Have mercy upon me, O Lord; for I

am weak: O Lord, heal me; for my bones are vexed. *Psalm 6:2*

Wait on the Lord: be of good courage, and He shall strengthen thine heart: wait, I say, on the Lord.
Psalm 27:14

Be of good courage, and He shall strengthen your heart, all ye that hope in the Lord. *Psalm 31:24*

Counsel is Mine, and sound wisdom: I am understanding; I have strength. *Proverbs 8:14*

Through wisdom is an house builded; and by understanding it is established:

And by knowledge shall the chambers be filled with all precious and pleasant riches.

A wise man is strong; yea, a man of knowledge increaseth strength.
Proverbs 24:3-5

Wisdom strengtheneth the wise

more than ten mighty men which are in the city. *Ecclesiastes 7:19*

If the iron be blunt, and he do not whet the edge, then must he put to more strength: but wisdom is profitable to direct. *Ecclesiastes 10:10*

Strengthen ye the weak hands, and confirm the feeble knees.
Isaiah 35:3

And being fully persuaded that, what He had promised, He was able also to perform. *Romans 4:21*

But God hath chosen the foolish things of the world to confound the wise; and God hath chosen the weak things of the world to confound the things which are mighty;
1 Corinthians 1:27

For to one is given by the Spirit the word of wisdom; to another the word of knowledge by the same Spirit;
1 Corinthians 12:8

And God is able to make all grace abound toward you; that ye, always having all sufficiency in all things, may abound to every good work:

2 Corinthians 9:8

And He said unto me, My grace is sufficient for thee: for My strength is made perfect in weakness. Most gladly therefore will I rather glory in my infirmities, that the power of Christ may rest upon me. *2 Corinthians 12:9*

If any of you lack wisdom, let him ask of God, that giveth to all men liberally, and upbraideth not; and it shall be given him. *James 1:5*

66

WHEN YOU FIND IT DIFFICULT TO BE THE SPIRITUAL LEADER IN YOUR HOME

For I know Him, that He will command His children and His household after Him, and they shall keep the way of the Lord, to do justice and judgment; that the Lord may bring upon Abraham that which He hath spoken of him. *Genesis 18:19*

And that thou mayest tell in the ears of thy son, and of thy son's son, what things I have wrought in Egypt, and My signs which I have done among them; that ye may know how that I am the Lord. *Exodus 10:2*

And thou shalt shew thy son in that day, saying, This is done because of that which the Lord did unto me when I came forth out of Egypt. *Exodus 13:8*

Only take heed to thyself, and keep thy soul diligently, lest thou forget the things which thine eyes have seen, and lest they depart from thy heart all the days of thy life: but teach them thy sons, and thy sons' sons;

Specially the day that thou stoodest before the Lord thy God in Horeb, when the Lord said unto me, Gather Me the people together, and I will make them hear My words, that they may learn to fear Me all the days that they shall live upon the earth, and that they may teach their children.

Deuteronomy 4:9,10

And thou shalt teach them diligently unto thy children, and shalt talk of them when thou sittest in thine house, and when thou walkest by the way, and when thou liest down, and when thou risest up. *Deuteronomy 6:7*

And the Lord commanded us to do all these statutes, to fear the Lord our God, for our good always, that He might preserve us alive, as it is at this day.

Deuteronomy 6:24

Therefore shall ye lay up these My words in your heart and in your soul, and bind them for a sign upon your hand, that they may be as frontlets between your eyes.

And ye shall teach them your children, speaking of them when thou sittest in thine house, and when thou walkest by the way, when thou liest down, and when thou risest up.

And thou shalt write them upon the door posts of thine house, and upon thy gates:

That your days may be multiplied, and the days of your children, in the land which the Lord sware unto your fathers to give them, as the days of heaven upon the earth.

Deuteronomy 11:18-21

For He established a testimony in

Jacob, and appointed a law in Israel, which He commanded our fathers, that they should make them known to their children:

That the generation to come might know them, even the children which should be born; who should arise and declare them to their children:

Psalm 78:5,6

A good man leaveth an inheritance to his children's children: and the wealth of the sinner is laid up for the just. *Proverbs 13:22*

Train up a child in the way he should go: and when he is old, he will not depart from it. *Proverbs 22:6*

Withhold not correction from the child: for if thou beatest him with the rod, he shall not die. *Proverbs 23:13*

The rod and reproof give wisdom: but a child left to himself bringeth his mother to shame. *Proverbs 29:15*

Correct thy son, and he shall give thee rest; yea, he shall give delight unto thy soul. *Proverbs 29:17*

The living, the living, he shall praise Thee, as I do this day: the father to the children shall make known Thy truth. *Isaiah 38:19*

Tell ye your children of it, and let your children tell their children, and their children another generation.

Joel 1:3

And he shall turn the heart of the fathers to the children, and the heart of the children to their fathers, lest I come and smite the earth with a curse.

Malachi 4:6

If a son shall ask bread of any of you that is a father, will he give him a stone? or if he ask a fish, will he for a fish give him a serpent?

Or if he shall ask an egg, will he offer him a scorpion?

If ye then, being evil, know how to

give good gifts unto your children: how much more shall your heavenly Father give the Holy Spirit to them that ask Him? *Luke 11:11-13*

Behold, the third time I am ready to come to you; and I will not be burdensome to you: for I seek not your's, but you: for the children ought not to lay up for the parents, but the parents for the children.
2 Corinthians 12:14

And, ye fathers, provoke not your children to wrath: but bring them up in the nurture and admonition of the Lord. *Ephesians 6:4*

Fathers, provoke not your children to anger, lest they be discouraged.
Colossians 3:21

As ye know how we exhorted and comforted and charged every one of you, as a father doth his children,
1 Thessalonians 2:11

One that ruleth well his own house, having his children in subjection with all gravity;

For if a man know not how to rule his own house, how shall he take care of the church of God?

Let the deacons be the husbands of one wife, ruling their children and their own houses well. *1 Timothy 3:4,5,12*

But if any provide not for his own, and specially for those of his own house, he hath denied the faith, and is worse than an infidel. *1 Timothy 5:8*

If ye endure chastening, God dealeth with you as with sons; for what son is he whom the father chasteneth not? *Hebrews 12:7*

67

WHEN A SPIRITUAL MENTOR FAILS

Keep me as the apple of the eye, hide me under the shadow of Thy wings,

From the wicked that oppress me, from my deadly enemies, who compass me about. *Psalm 17:8,9*

For in the time of trouble He shall hide me in His pavilion: in the secret of His tabernacle shall He hide me; He shall set me up upon a rock.

Psalm 27:5

Thou shalt hide them in the secret of Thy presence from the pride of man: Thou shalt keep them secretly in a pavilion from the strife of tongues.

Psalm 31:20

Thou art my hiding place; Thou shalt preserve me from trouble; Thou shalt compass me about with songs of deliverance. *Psalm 32:7*

My confusion is continually before me, and the shame of my face hath covered me,

For the voice of him that reproacheth and blasphemeth; by reason of the enemy and avenger.

All this is come upon us; yet have we not forgotten Thee, neither have we dealt falsely in Thy covenant.

Our heart is not turned back, neither have our steps declined from Thy way; *Psalm 44:15-18*

Behold, God is mine helper: the Lord is with them that uphold my soul. *Psalm 54:4*

From the end of the earth will I cry unto Thee, when my heart is overwhelmed: lead me to the rock that is higher than I.

For Thou hast been a shelter for

me, and a strong tower from the enemy.
Psalm 61:2,3

Hide not Thy face from me in the day when I am in trouble; incline Thine ear unto me: in the day when I call answer me speedily. *Psalm 102:2*

Thou art my hiding place and my shield: I hope in Thy word.
Psalm 119:114

Hear me speedily, O Lord: my spirit faileth: hide not Thy face from me, lest I be like unto them that go down into the pit.

Cause me to hear Thy lovingkindness in the morning; for in Thee do I trust: cause me to know the way wherein I should walk; for I lift up my soul unto Thee.

Deliver me, O Lord, from mine enemies: I flee unto Thee to hide me.

Teach me to do Thy will; for Thou art my God: Thy spirit is good; lead me into the land of uprightness.
Psalm 143:7-10

Quicken me, O Lord, for Thy name's sake: for Thy righteousness' sake bring my soul out of trouble.

Psalm 143:11

If thou seest the oppression of the poor, and violent perverting of judgment and justice in a province, marvel not at the matter: for He that is higher than the highest regardeth; and there be higher than they.

Ecclesiastes 5:8

Come, My people, enter thou into thy chambers, and shut thy doors about thee: hide thyself as it were for a little moment, until the indignation be overpast. *Isaiah 26:20*

And a man shall be as an hiding place from the wind, and a covert from the tempest; as rivers of water in a dry place, as the shadow of a great rock in a weary land. *Isaiah 32:2*

Judge not, and ye shall not be judged: condemn not, and ye shall not be condemned: forgive, and ye shall be forgiven: *Luke 6:37*

And forgive us our sins; for we also forgive every one that is indebted to us. And lead us not into temptation; but deliver us from evil. *Luke 11:4*

Then said Jesus, Father, forgive them; for they know not what they do. And they parted His raiment, and cast lots. *Luke 23:34*

Jesus saith unto him, Rise, take up thy bed, and walk. *John 5:8*

And be ye kind one to another, tenderhearted, forgiving one another, even as God for Christ's sake hath forgiven you. *Ephesians 4:32*

For the which cause I also suffer these things: nevertheless I am not ashamed: for I know whom I have believed, and am persuaded that He is able to keep that which I have committed unto Him against that day. *2 Timothy 1:12*

Who, when He was reviled, reviled not again; when He suffered, He threatened not; but committed Himself to Him that judgeth righteously:

1 Peter 2:23

Wherefore let them that suffer according to the will of God commit the keeping of their souls to Him in well-doing, as unto a faithful Creator.

1 Peter 4:19

Your Personal Needs

68

When You Need Personal Motivation

I had fainted, unless I had believed to see the goodness of the Lord in the land of the living.

Wait on the Lord: be of good courage, and He shall strengthen thine heart: wait, I say, on the Lord.

Psalm 27:13,14

Be of good courage, and He shall strengthen your heart, all ye that hope in the Lord. *Psalm 31:24*

For in Thee, O Lord, do I hope: Thou wilt hear, O Lord my God.

Psalm 38:15

And now, Lord, what wait I for? my hope is in Thee. *Psalm 39:7*

Why art thou cast down, O my soul? and why art thou disquieted within me? hope in God: for I shall yet praise Him, who is the health of my countenance, and my God. *Psalm 43:5*

For Thou art my hope, O Lord God: Thou art my trust from my youth.

But I will hope continually, and will yet praise Thee more and more.

Psalm 71:5,14

My soul fainteth for Thy salvation: but I hope in Thy word. *Psalm 119:81*

Lord, I have hoped for Thy salvation, and done Thy commandments.

My soul hath kept Thy testimonies;

and I love them exceedingly.
Psalm 119:166,167

Happy is he that hath the God of Jacob for his help, whose hope is in the Lord his God: *Psalm 146:5*

Trust in the Lord with all thine heart; and lean not unto thine own understanding. *Proverbs 3:5*

Hope deferred maketh the heart sick, but when the desire cometh, it is a tree of life. *Proverbs 13:12*

For surely there is an end; and thine expectation shall not be cut off.
Proverbs 23:18

So shall the knowledge of wisdom be unto thy soul: when thou hast found it, then there shall be a reward, and thy expectation shall not be cut off.
Proverbs 24:14

Blessed is the man that trusteth in the Lord, and whose hope the Lord is.
Jeremiah 17:7

The Lord is my portion, saith my soul; therefore will I hope in him.

It is good that a man should both hope and quietly wait for the salvation of the Lord. *Lamentations 3:24,26*

Jesus said unto him, If thou canst believe, all things are possible to him that believeth.

And straightway the father of the child cried out, and said with tears, Lord, I believe; help Thou mine unbelief. *Mark 9:23,24*

For verily I say unto you, That whosoever shall say unto this mountain, Be thou removed, and be thou cast into the sea; and shall not doubt in his heart, but shall believe that those things which he saith shall come to pass; he shall have whatsoever he saith.

Therefore I say unto you, What things soever ye desire, when ye pray, believe that ye receive them, and ye shall have them. *Mark 11:23,24*

Who against hope believed in hope, that he might become the father of many nations, according to that which was spoken, So shall thy seed be.

Romans 4:18

But if we hope for that we see not, then do we with patience wait for it.

Romans 8:25

Rejoicing in hope; patient in tribulation; continuing instant in prayer; *Romans 12:12*

For whatsoever things were written aforetime were written for our learning, that we through patience and comfort of the scriptures might have hope.

Now the God of hope fill you with all joy and peace in believing, that ye may abound in hope, through the power of the Holy Ghost. *Romans 15:4,13*

And take the helmet of salvation, and the sword of the Spirit, which is the word of God:

Praying always with all prayer and supplication in the Spirit, and watching thereunto with all perseverance and supplication for all saints;

Ephesians 6:17,18

Now faith is the substance of things hoped for, the evidence of things not seen. *Hebrews 11:1*

69

WHEN YOU NEED INNER PEACE

I will both lay me down in peace, and sleep: for Thou, Lord, only makest me dwell in safety. *Psalm 4:8*

What man is he that feareth the Lord? him shall he teach in the way that he shall choose.

His soul shall dwell at ease; and his seed shall inherit the earth.

Psalm 25:12,13

The Lord will give strength unto His people; the Lord will bless His people with peace. *Psalm 29:11*

Delight thyself also in the Lord; and He shall give thee the desires of thine heart.

But the meek shall inherit the

earth; and shall delight themselves in the abundance of peace.

Mark the perfect man, and behold the upright: for the end of that man is peace. *Psalm 37:4,11,37*

I will hear what God the Lord will speak: for He will speak peace unto His people, and to His saints: but let them not turn again to folly. *Psalm 85:8*

Great peace have they which love Thy law: and nothing shall offend them. *Psalm 119:165*

Better is an handful with quietness, than both the hands full with travail and vexation of spirit.
Ecclesiastes 4:6

For unto us a child is born, unto us a son is given: and the government shall be upon His shoulder: and His name shall be called Wonderful, Counsellor, The mighty God, The everlasting Father, The Prince of Peace.
Isaiah 9:6

And in that day thou shalt say, O Lord, I will praise Thee: though Thou wast angry with me, Thine anger is turned away, and Thou comfortedst me.

Behold, God is my salvation; I will trust, and not be afraid: for the Lord Jehovah is my strength and my song; He also is become my salvation.

Isaiah 12:1,2

Thou wilt keep him in perfect peace, whose mind is stayed on Thee: because he trusteth in Thee.

Isaiah 26:3

And a man shall be as an hiding place from the wind, and a covert from the tempest; as rivers of water in a dry place, as the shadow of a great rock in a weary land. *Isaiah 32:2*

Peace I leave with you, My peace I give unto you: not as the world giveth, give I unto you. Let not your heart be troubled, neither let it be afraid.

John 14:27

These things I have spoken unto you, that in Me ye might have peace. In the world ye shall have tribulation: but be of good cheer; I have overcome the world. *John 16:33*

For to be carnally minded is death; but to be spiritually minded is life and peace. *Romans 8:6*

For the kingdom of God is not meat and drink; but righteousness, and peace, and joy in the Holy Ghost. *Romans 14:17*

Now the God of hope fill you with all joy and peace in believing, that ye may abound in hope, through the power of the Holy Ghost. *Romans 15:13*

Grace be to you and peace from God the Father, and from our Lord Jesus Christ, *Galatians 1:3*

But the fruit of the Spirit is love, joy, peace, longsuffering, gentleness, goodness, faith, *Galatians 5:22*

For He is our peace, Who hath made both one, and hath broken down the middle wall of partition between us; *Ephesians 2:14*

And the peace of God, which

passeth all understanding, shall keep your hearts and minds through Christ Jesus.

Those things, which ye have both learned, and received, and heard, and seen in me, do: and the God of peace shall be with you. *Philippians 4:7,9*

And let the peace of God rule in your hearts, to the which also ye are called in one body; and be ye thankful.
Colossians 3:15

Now the Lord of peace Himself give you peace always by all means. The Lord be with you all.
2 Thessalonians 3:16

But the wisdom that is from above is first pure, then peaceable, gentle, and easy to be intreated, full of mercy and good fruits, without partiality, and without hypocrisy.

And the fruit of righteousness is sown in peace of them that make peace.
James 3:17,18

70

WHEN YOU NEED TO FORGIVE

The discretion of a man deferreth his anger; and it is his glory to pass over a transgression. *Proverbs 19:11*

Rejoice not when thine enemy falleth, and let not thine heart be glad when he stumbleth:

Say not, I will do so to him as he hath done to me: I will render to the man according to his work.

Proverbs 24:17,29

If thine enemy be hungry, give him bread to eat; and if he be thirsty, give him water to drink:

For thou shalt heap coals of fire upon his head, and the Lord shall reward thee. *Proverbs 25:21,22*

Also take no heed unto all words that are spoken; lest thou hear thy servant curse thee: *Ecclesiastes 7:21*

Blessed are the merciful: for they shall obtain mercy.

But I say unto you, That ye resist not evil: but whosoever shall smite thee on thy right cheek, turn to him the other also.

But I say unto you, Love your enemies, bless them that curse you, do good to them that hate you, and pray for them which despitefully use you, and persecute you;

For if ye love them which love you, what reward have ye? do not even the publicans the same?

Matthew 5:7,39,44,46

And forgive us our debts, as we forgive our debtors.

For if ye forgive men their trespasses, your heavenly Father will also forgive you:

But if ye forgive not men their trespasses, neither will your Father forgive your trespasses.

Matthew 6:12,14,15

Then came Peter to Him, and said, Lord, how oft shall my brother sin against me, and I forgive him? till seven times?

Jesus saith unto him, I say not unto thee, Until seven times: but, Until seventy times seven.

Matthew 18:21,22

And when ye stand praying, forgive, if ye have aught against any: that your Father also which is in heaven may forgive you your trespasses. *Mark 11:25*

Take heed to yourselves: If thy brother trespass against thee, rebuke him; and if he repent, forgive him.

And if he trespass against thee seven times in a day, and seven times in a day turn again to thee, saying, I repent; thou shalt forgive him.

Luke 17:3,4

Bless them which persecute you: bless, and curse not.

Recompense to no man evil for evil. Provide things honest in the sight of all men.

Dearly beloved, avenge not yourselves, but rather give place unto wrath: for it is written, Vengeance is mine; I will repay, saith the Lord.

Be not overcome of evil, but overcome evil with good.

Romans 12:14,17,19,21

And labour, working with our own hands: being reviled, we bless; being persecuted, we suffer it:

Being defamed, we intreat: we are made as the filth of the world, and are the offscouring of all things unto this day. *1 Corinthians 4:12,13*

And be ye kind one to another, tenderhearted, forgiving one another, even as God for Christ's sake hath forgiven you. *Ephesians 4:32*

Forbearing one another, and

forgiving one another, if any man have a quarrel against any: even as Christ forgave you, so also do ye.

Colossians 3:13

Not rendering evil for evil, or railing for railing: but contrariwise blessing; knowing that ye are thereunto called, that ye should inherit a blessing.

1 Peter 3:9

71

When You Need To Apologize

The meek will He guide in judgment: and the meek will He teach His way.
Psalm 25:9

Lord, my heart is not haughty, nor mine eyes lofty: neither do I exercise myself in great matters, or in things too high for me.

Surely I have behaved and quieted myself, as a child that is weaned of his mother: my soul is even as a weaned child.
Psalm 131:1,2

Though the Lord be high, yet hath He respect unto the lowly: but the proud He knoweth afar off.
Psalm 138:6

The Lord lifteth up the meek: He casteth the wicked down to the ground.
Psalm 147:6

Surely He scorneth the scorners: but He giveth grace unto the lowly.
Proverbs 3:34

When pride cometh, then cometh shame: but with the lowly is wisdom.
Proverbs 11:2

Better it is to be of an humble spirit with the lowly, than to divide the spoil with the proud. *Proverbs 16:19*

By humility and the fear of the Lord are riches, and honour, and life.
Proverbs 22:4

Let another man praise thee, and not thine own mouth; a stranger, and not thine own lips. *Proverbs 27:2*

Woe to Ariel, to Ariel, the city where David dwelt! add ye year to year; let them kill sacrifices. *Isaiah 29:1*

For thus saith the high and lofty One that inhabiteth eternity, whose name is Holy; I dwell in the high and holy place, with him also that is of a contrite and humble spirit, to revive the spirit of the humble, and to revive the heart of the contrite ones. *Isaiah 57:15*

For all those things hath Mine hand made, and all those things have been, saith the Lord: but to this man will I look, even to him that is poor and of a contrite spirit, and trembleth at My word. *Isaiah 66:2*

He hath shewed thee, O man, what is good; and what doth the Lord require of thee, but to do justly, and to love mercy, and to walk humbly with thy God? *Micah 6:8*

Blessed are the poor in spirit: for theirs is the kingdom of heaven.
Matthew 5:3

And Jesus called a little child unto Him, and set him in the midst of them,

And said, Verily I say unto you, Except ye be converted, and become as little children, ye shall not enter into the kingdom of heaven.

Whosoever therefore shall humble himself as this little child, the same is greatest in the kingdom of heaven.

Matthew 18:2-4

And whosoever shall exalt himself shall be abased; and he that shall humble himself shall be exalted.

Matthew 23:12

I tell you, this man went down to his house justified rather than the other: for every one that exalteth himself shall be abased; and he that humbleth himself shall be exalted.

Luke 18:14

For I say, through the grace given unto me, to every man that is among you, not to think of himself more highly than he ought to think; but to think soberly, according as God hath dealt to every man the measure of faith.

Romans 12:3

Wherefore let him that thinketh he standeth take heed lest he fall.
1 Corinthians 10:12

Charity suffereth long, and is kind; charity envieth not; charity vaunteth not itself, is not puffed up,
1 Corinthians 13:4

Let us not be desirous of vain glory, provoking one another, envying one another. *Galatians 5:26*

Let nothing be done through strife or vainglory; but in lowliness of mind let each esteem other better than themselves. *Philippians 2:3*

But He giveth more grace. Wherefore He saith, God resisteth the proud, but giveth grace unto the humble.

Humble yourselves in the sight of the Lord, and He shall lift you up.
James 4:6,10

Likewise, ye younger, submit

yourselves unto the elder. Yea, all of you be subject one to another, and be clothed with humility: for God resisteth the proud, and giveth grace to the humble.

Humble yourselves therefore under the mighty hand of God, that He may exalt you in due time:

1 Peter 5:5,6

72

When You Need Physical Healing

The Lord will strengthen him upon the bed of languishing: Thou wilt make all his bed in his sickness. *Psalm 41:3*

Cast thy burden upon the Lord, and He shall sustain thee: He shall never suffer the righteous to be moved. *Psalm 55:22*

My flesh and my heart faileth: but God is the strength of my heart, and my portion for ever. *Psalm 73:26*

Bless the Lord, O my soul: and all that is within me, bless His holy name.

Bless the Lord, O my soul, and forget not all His benefits:

Who forgiveth all thine iniquities; Who healeth all thy diseases;

Psalm 103:1-3

But He was wounded for our transgressions, He was bruised for our iniquities: the chastisement of our peace was upon Him; and with His stripes we are healed. *Isaiah 53:5*

For I will surely deliver thee, and thou shalt not fall by the sword, but thy life shall be for a prey unto thee: because thou hast put thy trust in Me, saith the Lord. *Jeremiah 39:18*

The Lord is good, a strong hold in the day of trouble; and He knoweth them that trust in Him. *Nahum 1:7*

Come unto me, all ye that labour and are heavy laden, and I will give you rest. *Matthew 11:28*

And when the Lord saw her, He had compassion on her, and said unto her, Weep not. *Luke 7:13*

And we know that all things work together for good to them that love God, to them who are the called according to His purpose. *Romans 8:28*

Blessed be God, even the Father of our Lord Jesus Christ, the Father of mercies, and the God of all comfort;

Who comforteth us in all our tribulation, that we may be able to comfort them which are in any trouble, by the comfort wherewith we ourselves are comforted of God.

For as the sufferings of Christ abound in us, so our consolation also aboundeth by Christ.

2 Corinthians 1:3-5

For which cause we faint not; but though our outward man perish, yet the inward man is renewed day by day.

For our light affliction, which is but for a moment, worketh for us a far more exceeding and eternal weight of glory; *2 Corinthians 4:16,17*

Nevertheless God, that comforteth

those that are cast down, comforted us by the coming of Titus;

2 Corinthians 7:6

Forasmuch then as the children are partakers of flesh and blood, He also Himself likewise took part of the same; that through death He might destroy him that had the power of death, that is, the devil;

And deliver them who through fear of death were all their lifetime subject to bondage. *Hebrews 2:14,15*

For in that He Himself hath suffered being tempted, He is able to succour them that are tempted.

Hebrews 2:18

For we have not an high priest which cannot be touched with the feeling of our infirmities; but was in all points tempted like as we are, yet without sin.

Let us therefore come boldly unto the throne of grace, that we may obtain mercy, and find grace to help in time of need. *Hebrews 4:15,16*

Let your conversation be without covetousness; and be content with such things as ye have: for He hath said, I will never leave thee, nor forsake thee.

So that we may boldly say, The Lord is my helper, and I will not fear what man shall do unto me.

Hebrews 13:5,6

Take, my brethren, the prophets, who have spoken in the name of the Lord, for an example of suffering affliction, and of patience. *James 5:10*

Beloved, think it not strange concerning the fiery trial which is to try you, as though some strange thing happened unto you:

But rejoice, inasmuch as ye are partakers of Christ's sufferings; that, when His glory shall be revealed, ye may be glad also with exceeding joy.

1 Peter 4:12,13

Who His own self bare our sins in His own body on the tree, that we, being dead to sins, should live unto righteousness: by Whose stripes ye were healed.

1 Peter 2:24

Casting all your care upon Him; for He careth for you.

Whom resist stedfast in the faith, knowing that the same afflictions are accomplished in your brethren that are in the world. *1 Peter 5:7,9*

73

When You Need Wisdom

Give therefore thy servant an understanding heart to judge thy people, that I may discern between good and bad: for who is able to judge this thy so great a people? *1 Kings 3:9*

I will bless the Lord, Who hath given me counsel: my reins also instruct me in the night seasons. *Psalm 16:7*

I am Thy servant; give me understanding, that I may know Thy testimonies.

It is time for Thee, Lord, to work: for they have made void Thy law.

The entrance of Thy words giveth light; it giveth understanding unto the simple.

I opened my mouth, and panted:

for I longed for Thy commandments.
Psalm 119:125,126,130,131

For the Lord giveth wisdom: out of His mouth cometh knowledge and understanding.

He layeth up sound wisdom for the righteous: He is a buckler to them that walk uprightly. *Proverbs 2:6,7*

Trust in the Lord with all thine heart; and lean not unto thine own understanding. *Proverbs 3:5*

Apply thine heart unto instruction, and thine ears to the words of knowledge.

Hear thou, my son, and be wise, and guide thine heart in the way.

Buy the truth, and sell it not; also wisdom, and instruction, and understanding. *Proverbs 23:12,19,23*

My son, eat thou honey, because it is good; and the honeycomb, which is sweet to thy taste: *Proverbs 24:13*

Thou shalt beat him with the rod, and shalt deliver his soul from hell.

Proverbs 23:14

For God giveth to a man that is good in His sight wisdom, and knowledge, and joy: but to the sinner He giveth travail, to gather and to heap up, that He may give to Him that is good before God. This also is vanity and vexation of spirit. *Ecclesiastes 2:26*

And thine ears shall hear a word behind thee, saying, This is the way, walk ye in it, when ye turn to the right hand, and when ye turn to the left.

Isaiah 30:21

For I will give you a mouth and wisdom, which all your adversaries shall not be able to gainsay nor resist.

Luke 21:15

Howbeit when He, the Spirit of truth, is come, He will guide you into all truth: for He shall not speak of Himself; but whatsoever He shall hear, that shall He speak: and He will shew you things to come.

He shall glorify me: for He shall receive of mine, and shall shew it unto you. *John 16:13,14*

For to one is given by the Spirit the word of wisdom; to another the word of knowledge by the same Spirit;

1 Corinthians 12:8

That the God of our Lord Jesus Christ, the Father of glory, may give unto you the Spirit of wisdom and revelation in the knowledge of Him:

The eyes of your understanding being enlightened; that ye may know what is the hope of His calling, and what the riches of the glory of His inheritance in the saints,

Ephesians 1:17,18

See then that ye walk circumspectly, not as fools, but as wise,

Ephesians 5:15

For this cause we also, since the

day we heard it, do not cease to pray for you, and to desire that ye might be filled with the knowledge of His will in all wisdom and spiritual understanding;

That ye might walk worthy of the Lord unto all pleasing, being fruitful in every good work, and increasing in the knowledge of God; *Colossians 1:9,10*

In Whom are hid all the treasures of wisdom and knowledge.

Colossians 2:3

Walk in wisdom toward them that are without, redeeming the time.

Colossians 4:5

For God hath not given us the spirit of fear; but of power, and of love, and of a sound mind. *2 Timothy 1:7*

If any of you lack wisdom, let him ask of God, that giveth to all men liberally, and upbraideth not; and it shall be given him. *James 1:5*

Who is a wise man and endued with knowledge among you? let him shew out of a good conversation his works with meekness of wisdom.

But the wisdom that is from above is first pure, then peaceable, gentle, and easy to be intreated, full of mercy and good fruits, without partiality, and without hypocrisy. *James 3:13,17*

74

WHEN YOU FAIL TO MEET YOUR PERSONAL EXPECTATIONS

And the Lord said unto Moses, Depart, and go up hence, thou and the people which thou hast brought up out of the land of Egypt, unto the land which I sware unto Abraham, to Isaac, and to Jacob, saying, Unto thy seed will I give it:

And I will send an angel before thee; and I will drive out the Canaanite, the Amorite, and the Hittite, and the Perizzite, the Hivite, and the Jebusite:

Exodus 33:1,2

And they commanded the people, saying, When ye see the ark of the covenant of the Lord your God, and the priests the Levites bearing it, then ye shall remove from your place, and go after it. *Joshua 3:3*

Let Thine ear now be attentive, and Thine eyes open, that Thou mayest hear the prayer of Thy servant, which I pray before Thee now, day and night, for the children of Israel Thy servants, and confess the sins of the children of Israel, which we have sinned against Thee: both I and my father's house have sinned. *Nehemiah 1:6*

Moreover thou leddest them in the day by a cloudy pillar; and in the night by a pillar of fire, to give them light in the way wherein they should go.

Yet Thou in Thy manifold mercies forsookest them not in the wilderness: the pillar of the cloud departed not from them by day, to lead them in the way; neither the pillar of fire by night, to shew them light, and the way wherein they should go. *Nehemiah 9:12,19*

Thou shalt also decree a thing, and

it shall be established unto thee: and the light shall shine upon thy ways.

Or darkness, that thou canst not see; and abundance of waters cover thee. *Job 22:28,11*

Lo, all these things worketh God oftentimes with man,

To bring back his soul from the pit, to be enlightened with the light of the living. *Job 33:29,30*

For thou wilt light my candle: the Lord my God will enlighten my darkness. *Psalm 18:28*

Teach me Thy way, O Lord, and lead me in a plain path, because of mine enemies. *Psalm 27:11*

I will instruct thee and teach thee in the way which thou shalt go: I will guide thee with Mine eye. *Psalm 32:8*

For with Thee is the fountain of life: in Thy light shall we see light. *Psalm 36:9*

O send out Thy light and Thy truth: let them lead me; let them bring me unto Thy holy hill, and to Thy tabernacles. *Psalm 43:3*

So teach us to number our days, that we may apply our hearts unto wisdom. *Psalm 90:12*

Unto the upright there ariseth light in the darkness: He is gracious, and full of compassion, and righteous.
Psalm 112:4

Thy word is a lamp unto my feet, and a light unto my path.

The entrance of Thy words giveth light; it giveth understanding unto the simple. *Psalm 119:105,130*

Trust in the Lord with all thine heart; and lean not unto thine own understanding.

In all thy ways acknowledge Him, and He shall direct thy paths.
Proverbs 3:5,6

The simple believeth every word:

but the prudent man looketh well to his going. *Proverbs 14:15*

The spirit of man is the candle of the Lord, searching all the inward parts of the belly. *Proverbs 20:27*

A prudent man foreseeth the evil, and hideth himself: but the simple pass on, and are punished. *Proverbs 22:3*

And be not conformed to this world: but be ye transformed by the renewing of your mind, that ye may prove what is that good, and acceptable, and perfect, will of God. *Romans 12:2*

But let every man prove his own work, and then shall he have rejoicing in himself alone, and not in another. *Galatians 6:4*

Wherefore He saith, Awake thou that sleepest, and arise from the dead, and Christ shall give thee light. *Ephesians 5:14*

Prove all things; hold fast that which is good. *1 Thessalonians 5:21*

75

WHEN YOU FEEL INCAPABLE OF ACHIEVING YOUR DREAMS AND GOALS

But if from thence thou shalt seek the Lord thy God, thou shalt find Him, if thou seek Him with all thy heart and with all thy soul.

For the Lord thy God is a merciful God; He will not forsake thee, neither destroy thee, nor forget the covenant of thy fathers which He sware unto them.

Deuteronomy 4:29,31

In thee, O Lord, do I put my trust; let me never be ashamed: deliver me in Thy righteousness.

Bow down Thine ear to me; deliver me speedily: be Thou my strong rock, for an house of defence to save me.

For Thou art my rock and my fortress; therefore for Thy name's sake lead me, and guide me.

Pull me out of the net that they have laid privily for me: for Thou art my strength.

Into Thine hand I commit my spirit: Thou hast redeemed me, O Lord God of truth. *Psalm 31:1-5*

The Lord is nigh unto them that are of a broken heart; and saveth such as be of a contrite spirit. *Psalm 34:18*

Create in me a clean heart, O God; and renew a right spirit within me.

Cast me not away from Thy presence; and take not Thy Holy Spirit from me.

Restore unto me the joy of Thy salvation; and uphold me with Thy free Spirit. *Psalm 51:10-12*

The sacrifices of God are a broken spirit: a broken and a contrite heart, O

God, Thou wilt not despise.

Psalm 51:17

But as for me, my feet were almost gone; my steps had well nigh slipped.

So foolish was I, and ignorant: I was as a beast before thee.

Nevertheless I am continually with thee: Thou hast holden me by my right hand.

Thou shalt guide me with Thy counsel, and afterward receive me to glory.

Whom have I in heaven but Thee? and there is none upon earth that I desire beside Thee.

My flesh and my heart faileth: but God is the strength of my heart, and my portion for ever. *Psalm 73:2,22-26*

He healeth the broken in heart, and bindeth up their wounds.

Psalm 147:3

And Peter remembered the word of Jesus, which said unto him, Before the cock crow, thou shalt deny Me thrice.

And he went out, and wept bitterly.

Matthew 26:75

Brethren, if a man be overtaken in a fault, ye which are spiritual, restore such an one in the spirit of meekness; considering thyself, lest thou also be tempted.

Bear ye one another's burdens, and so fulfil the law of Christ.

Galatians 6:1,2

Humble yourselves in the sight of the Lord, and He shall lift you up.

James 4:10

If we confess our sins, He is faithful and just to forgive us our sins, and to cleanse us from all unrighteousness. *1 John 1:9*

76

WHEN YOU FEEL LONELY AND UNAPPRECIATED

And Jacob was left alone; and there wrestled a man with him until the breaking of the day. *Genesis 32:24*

And the Lord, He it is that doth go before thee; He will be with thee, He will not fail thee, neither forsake thee: fear not, neither be dismayed.
Deuteronomy 31:8

The eternal God is thy refuge, and underneath are the everlasting arms: and He shall thrust out the enemy from before thee; and shall say, Destroy them. *Deuteronomy 33:27*

In my distress I called upon the Lord, and cried to my God: and He did hear my voice out of His temple, and my cry did enter into His ears.

2 Samuel 22:7

And they that know Thy name will put their trust in Thee: for Thou, Lord, hast not forsaken them that seek Thee.

Psalm 9:10

When my father and my mother forsake me, then the Lord will take me up. *Psalm 27:10*

For His anger endureth but a moment; in His favour is life: weeping may endure for a night, but joy cometh in the morning. *Psalm 30:5*

For I said in my haste, I am cut off from before Thine eyes: nevertheless Thou heardest the voice of my supplications when I cried unto Thee.

Psalm 31:22

The Lord is nigh unto them that are of a broken heart; and saveth such as be of a contrite spirit. *Psalm 34:18*

God is our refuge and strength, a very present help in trouble.

Psalm 46:1

Be merciful unto me, O God, be merciful unto me: for my soul trusteth in Thee: yea, in the shadow of Thy wings will I make my refuge, until these calamities be overpast.

Psalm 57:1

In God is my salvation and my glory: the rock of my strength, and my refuge, is in God.

Trust in Him at all times; ye people, pour out your heart before Him: God is a refuge for us. *Psalm 62:7,8*

Be Thou my strong habitation, whereunto I may continually resort: Thou hast given commandment to save me; for Thou art my rock and my fortress. *Psalm 71:3*

But the Lord is my defence; and my God is the rock of my refuge.

Psalm 94:22

I watch, and am as a sparrow alone upon the house top. *Psalm 102:7*

I looked on my right hand, and beheld, but there was no man that would know me: refuge failed me; no man cared for my soul.

I cried unto thee, O Lord: I said, Thou art my refuge and my portion in the land of the living. *Psalm 142:4,5*

The Lord is nigh unto all them that call upon Him, to all that call upon Him in truth. *Psalm 145:18*

And the work of righteousness shall be peace; and the effect of righteousness quietness and assurance for ever. *Isaiah 32:17*

He giveth power to the faint; and to them that have no might He increaseth strength. *Isaiah 40:29*

It is good that a man should both hope and quietly wait for the salvation of the Lord. *Lamentations 3:26*

Rejoicing in hope; patient in tribulation; continuing instant in prayer; *Romans 12:12*

Now the God of hope fill you with all joy and peace in believing, that ye may abound in hope, through the power of the Holy Ghost. *Romans 15:13*

Let your conversation be without covetousness; and be content with such things as ye have: for He hath said, I will never leave thee, nor forsake thee. *Hebrews 13:5*

Draw nigh to God, and He will draw nigh to you. Cleanse your hands, ye sinners; and purify your hearts, ye double-minded. *James 4:8*

77

WHEN YOU NEED TO OVERCOME ANGER

Blessed is the man that walketh not in the counsel of the ungodly, nor standeth in the way of sinners, nor sitteth in the seat of the scornful.

Psalm 1:1

I will both lay me down in peace, and sleep: for Thou, Lord, only makest me dwell in safety. *Psalm 4:8*

Delight thyself also in the Lord; and He shall give thee the desires of thine heart.

Commit thy way unto the Lord; trust also in Him; and He shall bring it to pass. *Psalm 37:4,5*

The discretion of a man deferreth his anger; and it is his glory to pass over a transgression. *Proverbs 19:11*

He that hath no rule over his own spirit is like a city that is broken down, and without walls. *Proverbs 25:28*

Better is the end of a thing than the beginning thereof: and the patient in spirit is better than the proud in spirit.

Be not hasty in thy spirit to be angry: for anger resteth in the bosom of fools. *Ecclesiastes 7:8,9*

Behold, God is my salvation; I will trust, and not be afraid: for the Lord Jehovah is my strength and my song; He also is become my salvation.

Isaiah 12:2

Thou wilt keep him in perfect peace, whose mind is stayed on Thee: because he trusteth in Thee.

Trust ye in the Lord for ever: for in the Lord Jehovah is everlasting strength: *Isaiah 26:3,4*

Blessed are the peacemakers: for they shall be called the children of God.
Matthew 5:9

Peace I leave with you, My peace I give unto you: not as the world giveth, give I unto you. Let not your heart be troubled, neither let it be afraid.
John 14:27

But the fruit of the Spirit is love, joy, peace, longsuffering, gentleness, goodness, faith,

Meekness, temperance: against such there is no law. *Galatians 5:22,23*

Be ye angry, and sin not: let not the sun go down upon your wrath:
Ephesians 4:26

Do all things without murmurings and disputings: *Philippians 2:14*

But now ye also put off all these; anger, wrath, malice, blasphemy, filthy communication out of your mouth.

Lie not one to another, seeing that ye have put off the old man with his deeds; *Colossians 3:8,9*

I will therefore that men pray every where, lifting up holy hands, without wrath and doubting.

1 Timothy 2:8

Wherefore, my beloved brethren, let every man be swift to hear, slow to speak, slow to wrath:

For the wrath of man worketh not the righteousness of God.

Wherefore lay apart all filthiness and superfluity of naughtiness, and receive with meekness the engrafted word, which is able to save your souls.

James 1:19-21

78

WHEN YOU NEED TO OVERCOME RESENTMENT

Wherefore is light given to him that is in misery, and life unto the bitter in soul;

Which long for death, but it cometh not; and dig for it more than for hid treasures; *Job 3:20,21*

Therefore I will not refrain my mouth; I will speak in the anguish of my spirit; I will complain in the bitterness of my soul. *Job 7:11*

But man dieth, and wasteth away: yea, man giveth up the ghost, and where is he? *Job 14:10*

Even to-day is my complaint

bitter: my stroke is heavier than my groaning.

Oh that I knew where I might find Him! that I might come even to His seat!

I would order my cause before Him, and fill my mouth with arguments.

I would know the words which He would answer me, and understand what He would say unto me.

Will He plead against me with His great power? No; but He would put strength in me.

There the righteous might dispute with Him; so should I be delivered for ever from my judge.

Behold, I go forward, but He is not there; and backward, but I cannot perceive Him:

On the left hand, where He doth work, but I cannot behold Him: He hideth Himself on the right hand, that I cannot see Him:

But He knoweth the way that I take: when He hath tried me, I shall come forth as gold. *Job 23:2-10*

Behold, for peace I had great bitterness: but Thou hast in love to my soul delivered it from the pit of corruption: for Thou hast cast all my sins behind Thy back. *Isaiah 38:17*

For I perceive that thou art in the gall of bitterness, and in the bond of iniquity. *Acts 8:23*

Let all bitterness, and wrath, and anger, and clamour, and evil speaking, be put away from you, with all malice:
Ephesians 4:31

Forbearing one another, and forgiving one another, if any man have a quarrel against any: even as Christ forgave you, so also do ye.

Husbands, love your wives, and be not bitter against them.
Colossians 3:13,19

Looking diligently lest any man fail of the grace of God; lest any root of bitterness springing up trouble you, and thereby many be defiled;
Hebrews 12:15

Doth a fountain send forth at the same place sweet water and bitter?

Can the fig tree, my brethren, bear olive berries? either a vine, figs? so can no fountain both yield salt water and fresh.

Who is a wise man and endued with knowledge among you? let him shew out of a good conversation his works with meekness of wisdom.

But if ye have bitter envying and strife in your hearts, glory not, and lie not against the truth.

This wisdom descendeth not from above, but is earthly, sensual, devilish.

For where envying and strife is, there is confusion and every evil work.

But the wisdom that is from above is first pure, then peaceable, gentle, and easy to be entreated, full of mercy and good fruits, without partiality, and without hypocrisy.

And the fruit of righteousness is sown in peace of them that make peace.

James 3:11-18

79

WHEN YOU NEED TO OVERCOME ENVY OR JEALOUSY

For wrath killeth the foolish man, and envy slayeth the silly one.

I have seen the foolish taking root: but suddenly I cursed his habitation.

Job 5:2,3

Fret not thyself because of evildoers, neither be thou envious against the workers of iniquity.

Rest in the Lord, and wait patiently for Him: fret not thyself because of him who prospereth in his way, because of the man who bringeth wicked devices to pass. *Psalm 37:1,7*

Be not thou afraid when one is

made rich, when the glory of his house is increased; *Psalm 49:16*

For I was envious at the foolish, when I saw the prosperity of the wicked.

When I thought to know this, it was too painful for me; *Psalm 73:3,16*

Wrath is cruel, and anger is outrageous; but who is able to stand before envy? *Proverbs 27:4*

Again, I considered all travail, and every right work, that for this a man is envied of his neighbour. This is also vanity and vexation of spirit.

Ecclesiastes 4:4

Set me as a seal upon thine heart, as a seal upon thine arm: for love is strong as death; jealousy is cruel as the grave: the coals thereof are coals of fire, which hath a most vehement flame.

Song of Solomon 8:6

Therefore, as I live, saith the Lord

God, I will even do according to thine anger, and according to thine envy which thou hast used out of thy hatred against them; and I will make Myself known among them, when I have judged thee. *Ezekiel 35:11*

Let us walk honestly, as in the day; not in rioting and drunkenness, not in chambering and wantonness, not in strife and envying. *Romans 13:13*

For ye are yet carnal: for whereas there is among you envying, and strife, and divisions, are ye not carnal, and walk as men? *1 Corinthians 3:3*

Charity suffereth long, and is kind; charity envieth not; charity vaunteth not itself, is not puffed up,
1 Corinthians 13:4

Now the works of the flesh are manifest, which are these; Adultery, fornication, uncleanness, lasciviousness,

Idolatry, witchcraft, hatred,

variance, emulations, wrath, strife, seditions, heresies,

Envyings, murders, drunkenness, revellings, and such like: of the which I tell you before, as I have also told you in time past, that they which do such things shall not inherit the kingdom of God.

Let us not be desirous of vain glory, provoking one another, envying one another. *Galatians 5:19-21,26*

For we ourselves also were sometimes foolish, disobedient, deceived, serving divers lusts and pleasures, living in malice and envy, hateful, and hating one another.
Titus 3:3

But if ye have bitter envying and strife in your hearts, glory not, and lie not against the truth. *James 3:14*

Do ye think that the scripture saith in vain, The spirit that dwelleth in us lusteth to envy? *James 4:5*

Grudge not one against another, brethren, lest ye be condemned: behold, the judge standeth before the door.

James 5:9

Wherefore laying aside all malice, and all guile, and hypocrisies, and envies, and all evil speakings,

1 Peter 2:1

80

WHEN YOU FEEL ANXIOUS ABOUT YOUR ADVANCING AGE

And thou shalt go to thy fathers in peace; thou shalt be buried in a good old age. *Genesis 15:15*

And Jacob said unto Pharaoh, The days of the years of my pilgrimage are an hundred and thirty years: few and evil have the days of the years of my life been, and have not attained unto the days of the years of the life of my fathers in the days of their pilgrimage. *Genesis 47:9*

And Moses was an hundred and twenty years old when he died: his eye was not dim, nor his natural force abated. *Deuteronomy 34:7*

And he died in a good old age, full of days, riches, and honour: and Solomon his son reigned in his stead.

1 Chronicles 29:28

Thou shalt come to thy grave in a full age, like as a shock of corn cometh in in his season. *Job 5:26*

And thine age shall be clearer than the noonday; thou shalt shine forth, thou shalt be as the morning.

Job 11:17

With the ancient is wisdom; and in length of days understanding.

Job 12:12

And Elihu the son of Barachel the Buzite answered and said, I am young, and ye are very old; wherefore I was afraid, and durst not shew you mine opinion.

I said, Days should speak, and multitude of years should teach wisdom.

But there is a spirit in man: and

the inspiration of the Almighty giveth them understanding.

Great men are not always wise: neither do the aged understand judgment. *Job 32:6-9*

So Job died, being old and full of days. *Job 42:17*

Surely goodness and mercy shall follow me all the days of my life: and I will dwell in the house of the Lord for ever. *Psalm 23:6*

One thing have I desired of the Lord, that will I seek after; that I may dwell in the house of the Lord all the days of my life, to behold the beauty of the Lord, and to inquire in His temple. *Psalm 27:4*

The Lord knoweth the days of the upright: and their inheritance shall be for ever. *Psalm 37:18*

Lord, make me to know mine end, and the measure of my days, what it is;

that I may know how frail I am.

Behold, thou hast made my days as an handbreadth; and mine age is as nothing before thee: verily every man at his best state is altogether vanity.

Psalm 39:4,5

Cast me not off in the time of old age; forsake me not when my strength faileth.

Now also when I am old and greyheaded, O God, forsake me not; until I have shewed Thy strength unto this generation, and Thy power to every one that is to come. *Psalm 71:9,18*

The days of our years are threescore years and ten; and if by reason of strength they be fourscore years, yet is their strength labour and sorrow; for it is soon cut off, and we fly away. *Psalm 90:10*

They shall still bring forth fruit in old age; they shall be fat and flourishing; *Psalm 92:14*

Both young men, and maidens; old

men, and children:

Let them praise the name of the Lord: for His name alone is excellent; His glory is above the earth and heaven. *Psalm 148:12,13*

And even to your old age I am he; and even to hoar hairs will I carry you: I have made, and I will bear; even I will carry, and will deliver you. *Isaiah 46:4*

And she was a widow of about fourscore and four years, which departed not from the temple, but served God with fastings and prayers night and day. *Luke 2:37*

That the aged men be sober, grave, temperate, sound in faith, in charity, in patience. *Titus 2:2*

Yet for love's sake I rather beseech thee, being such an one as Paul the aged, and now also a prisoner of Jesus Christ.

I beseech thee for my son Onesimus, whom I have begotten in my bonds: *Philemon 1:9,10*

81

WHEN YOU FEEL USED

For Thou hast girded me with strength to battle: them that rose up against me hast Thou subdued under me.
2 Samuel 22:40

And they were helped against them, and the Hagarites were delivered into their hand, and all that were with them: for they cried to God in the battle, and He was intreated of them; because they put their trust in Him.
1 Chronicles 5:20

Blessed is the man that walketh not in the counsel of the ungodly, nor standeth in the way of sinners, nor sitteth in the seat of the scornful.

But his delight is in the law of the Lord; and in His law doth he meditate day and night.

And he shall be like a tree planted by the rivers of water, that bringeth forth his fruit in his season; his leaf also shall not wither; and whatsoever he doeth shall prosper. *Psalm 1:1-3*

But Thou, O Lord, art a shield for me; my glory, and the lifter up of mine head.

I will not be afraid of ten thousands of people, that have set themselves against me round about.

Psalm 3:3,6

For Thou hast girded me with strength unto the battle: Thou hast subdued under me those that rose up against me.

He delivereth me from mine enemies: yea, Thou liftest me up above those that rise up against me: Thou hast delivered me from the violent man.

Psalm 18:39,48

He hath delivered my soul in peace from the battle that was against me:

for there were many with me.

Psalm 55:18

Save me, O God; for the waters are come in unto my soul.

I sink in deep mire, where there is no standing: I am come into deep waters, where the floods overflow me.

I am weary of my crying: my throat is dried: mine eyes fail while I wait for my God.

Let not the waterflood overflow me, neither let the deep swallow me up, and let not the pit shut her mouth upon me. *Psalm 69:1-3,15*

O God the Lord, the strength of my salvation, Thou hast covered my head in the day of battle. *Psalm 140:7*

The horse is prepared against the day of battle: but safety is of the Lord.

Proverbs 21:31

In that day shall the Lord of hosts be for a crown of glory, and for a diadem of beauty, unto the residue of His people, *Isaiah 28:5*

When thou passest through the waters, I will be with thee; and through the rivers, they shall not overflow thee: when thou walkest through the fire, thou shalt not be burned; neither shall the flame kindle upon thee.

Isaiah 43:2

Thou art my battle axe and weapons of war: for with Thee will I break in pieces the nations, and with Thee will I destroy kingdoms;

Jeremiah 51:20

But I have prayed for thee, that thy faith fail not: and when thou art converted, strengthen thy brethren.

Luke 22:32

For we would not, brethren, have you ignorant of our trouble which came to us in Asia, that we were pressed out of measure, above strength, insomuch that we despaired even of life:

But we had the sentence of death

in ourselves, that we should not trust in ourselves, but in God which raiseth the dead:

Who delivered us from so great a death, and doth deliver: in Whom we trust that He will yet deliver us;

2 Corinthians 1:8-10

That He would grant you, according to the riches of His glory, to be strengthened with might by His Spirit in the inner man;

Ephesians 3:16

I can do all things through Christ which strengtheneth me.

Philippians 4:13

Strengthened with all might, according to His glorious power, unto all patience and longsuffering with joyfulness;

Colossians 1:11

I know thy works: behold, I have set before thee an open door, and no man can shut it: for thou hast a little strength, and hast kept My word, and hast not denied My name.

To him that overcometh will I grant to sit with Me in My throne, even as I also overcame, and am set down with My Father in His throne.

He that hath an ear, let him hear what the Spirit saith unto the churches.

Revelation 3:8,21,22

82

WHEN YOU FEEL DEPRESSED

Shew me Thy ways, O Lord; teach me Thy paths.

Lead me in Thy truth, and teach me: for Thou art the God of my salvation; on Thee do I wait all the day.

Psalm 25:4,5

I sought the Lord, and He heard me, and delivered me from all my fears.

They looked unto Him, and were lightened: and their faces were not ashamed.

This poor man cried, and the Lord heard Him, and saved Him out of all His troubles.

The angel of the Lord encampeth round about them that fear Him, and delivereth them. *Psalm 34:4-7*

Behold, as the eyes of servants look unto the hand of their masters, and as the eyes of a maiden unto the hand of her mistress; so our eyes wait upon the Lord our God, until that He have mercy upon us. *Psalm 123:2*

Trust in the Lord with all thine heart; and lean not unto thine own understanding. *Proverbs 3:5*

Let thine eyes look right on, and let thine eyelids look straight before thee.

Ponder the path of thy feet, and let all thy ways be established.

Turn not to the right hand nor to the left: remove thy foot from evil.

Proverbs 4:25-27

The integrity of the upright shall guide them: but the perverseness of transgressors shall destroy them.

Proverbs 11:3

A man's heart deviseth his way: but the Lord directeth his steps.

Proverbs 16:9

A wicked man hardeneth his face: but as for the upright, He directeth his way. *Proverbs 21:29*

If the iron be blunt, and he do not whet the edge, then must he put to more strength: but wisdom is profitable to direct. *Ecclesiastes 10:10*

For the Lord God will help me; therefore shall I not be confounded: therefore have I set my face like a flint, and I know that I shall not be ashamed. *Isaiah 50:7*

O Lord, I know that the way of man is not in himself: it is not in man that walketh to direct his steps. *Jeremiah 10:23*

The Lord is good unto them that wait for Him, to the soul that seeketh Him.

It is good that a man should both hope and quietly wait for the salvation of the Lord. *Lamentations 3:25,26*

Therefore I will look unto the Lord; I will wait for the God of my salvation: my God will hear me. *Micah 7:7*

And when He had sent the multitudes away, He went up into a mountain apart to pray: and when the evening was come, He was there alone.
Matthew 14:23

And He said unto them, Come ye yourselves apart into a desert place, and rest a while: for there were many coming and going, and they had no leisure so much as to eat. *Mark 6:31*

Therefore, my beloved brethren, be ye stedfast, unmoveable, always abounding in the work of the Lord, forasmuch as ye know that your labour is not in vain in the Lord.
1 Corinthians 15:58

Watch ye, stand fast in the faith, quit you like men, be strong.
1 Corinthians 16:13

And let us not be weary in well doing: for in due season we shall reap, if we faint not. *Galatians 6:9*

But ye, brethren, be not weary in well doing. *2 Thessalonians 3:13*

If any of you lack wisdom, let him ask of God, that giveth to all men liberally, and upbraideth not; and it shall be given him.

A double-minded man is unstable in all his ways. *James 1:5,8*

Wherefore gird up the loins of your mind, be sober, and hope to the end for the grace that is to be brought unto you at the revelation of Jesus Christ;

1 Peter 1:13

83

WHEN YOU FACE SEXUAL TEMPTATION

And the Lord said unto satan, Hast thou considered My servant Job, that there is none like him in the earth, a perfect and an upright man, one that feareth God, and escheweth evil? and still he holdeth fast his integrity, although thou movedst Me against him, to destroy him without cause. *Job 2:3*

All the while my breath is in me, and the spirit of God is in my nostrils;

My lips shall not speak wickedness, nor my tongue utter deceit.
Job 27:3,4

God forbid that I should justify you: till I die I will not remove mine integrity from me.

My righteousness I hold fast, and will not let it go: my heart shall not reproach me so long as I live.

Job 27:5,6

Blessed is the man that walketh not in the counsel of the ungodly, nor standeth in the way of sinners, nor sitteth in the seat of the scornful.

Psalm 1:1

The Lord shall judge the people: judge me, O Lord, according to my righteousness, and according to mine integrity that is in me. *Psalm 7:8*

Let integrity and uprightness preserve me; for I wait on Thee.

Psalm 25:21

Judge me, O Lord; for I have walked in mine integrity: I have trusted also in the Lord; therefore I shall not slide.

Gather not my soul with sinners, nor my life with bloody men:

In whose hands is mischief, and their right hand is full of bribes.

But as for me, I will walk in mine integrity: redeem me, and be merciful unto me. *Psalm 26:1,9-11*

The integrity of the upright shall guide them: but the perverseness of transgressors shall destroy them.
Proverbs 11:3

Better is the poor that walketh in his integrity, than he that is perverse in his lips, and is a fool. *Proverbs 19:1*

The just man walketh in his integrity: his children are blessed after him. *Proverbs 20:7*

And lead us not into temptation, but deliver us from evil: For Thine is the kingdom, and the power, and the glory, for ever. Amen. *Matthew 6:13*

Watch and pray, that ye enter not into temptation: the spirit indeed is willing, but the flesh is weak.
Matthew 26:41

And the cares of this world, and

the deceitfulness of riches, and the lusts of other things entering in, choke the word, and it becometh unfruitful.

Mark 4:19

There hath no temptation taken you but such as is common to man: but God is faithful, Who will not suffer you to be tempted above that ye are able; but will with the temptation also make a way to escape, that ye may be able to bear it. *1 Corinthians 10:13*

But have renounced the hidden things of dishonesty, not walking in craftiness, nor handling the word of God deceitfully; but by manifestation of the truth commending ourselves to every man's conscience in the sight of God. *2 Corinthians 4:2*

That ye put off concerning the former conversation the old man, which is corrupt according to the deceitful lusts; *Ephesians 4:22*

For in that He Himself hath

suffered being tempted, He is able to succour them that are tempted.

Hebrews 2:18

But exhort one another daily, while it is called To-day; lest any of you be hardened through the deceitfulness of sin. *Hebrews 3:13*

Let no man say when he is tempted, I am tempted of God: for God cannot be tempted with evil, neither tempteth He any man:

But every man is tempted, when he is drawn away of his own lust, and enticed.

Then when lust hath conceived, it bringeth forth sin: and sin, when it is finished, bringeth forth death.

Do not err, my beloved brethren.

James 1:13-16

The Lord knoweth how to deliver the godly out of temptations, and to reserve the unjust unto the day of judgment to be punished: *2 Peter 2:9*

84

WHEN YOU FEEL GUILTY

But if from thence thou shalt seek the Lord thy God, thou shalt find Him, if thou seek Him with all thy heart and with all thy soul. *Deuteronomy 4:29*

And thou shalt return and obey the voice of the Lord, and do all His commandments which I command thee this day.

And the Lord thy God will make thee plenteous in every work of thine hand, in the fruit of thy body, and in the fruit of thy cattle, and in the fruit of thy land, for good: for the Lord will again rejoice over thee for good, as He rejoiced over thy fathers:

If thou shalt hearken unto the voice of the Lord thy God, to keep His commandments and His statutes which are written in this book of the law, and if thou turn unto the Lord thy God with all thine heart, and with all thy soul.

Deuteronomy 30:8-10

And David's heart smote him after that he had numbered the people. And David said unto the Lord, I have sinned greatly in that I have done: and now, I beseech Thee, O Lord, take away the iniquity of Thy servant; for I have done very foolishly. *2 Samuel 24:10*

If My people, which are called by My name, shall humble themselves, and pray, and seek My face, and turn from their wicked ways; then will I hear from heaven, and will forgive their sin, and will heal their land.

2 Chronicles 7:14

But if ye turn unto Me, and keep My commandments, and do them; though there were of you cast out unto the uttermost part of the heaven, yet will I gather them from thence, and will bring them unto the place that I have chosen to set My name there.

Nehemiah 1:9

If iniquity be in thine hand, put it far away, and let not wickedness dwell in thy tabernacles.

For then shalt thou lift up thy face without spot; yea, thou shalt be stedfast, and shalt not fear:

Job 11:14,15

The sacrifices of God are a broken spirit: a broken and a contrite heart, O God, Thou wilt not despise.

Psalm 51:17

So foolish was I, and ignorant: I was as a beast before Thee.

Nevertheless I am continually with Thee: Thou hast holden me by my right hand.

Thou shalt guide me with Thy counsel, and afterward receive me to glory. *Psalm 73:22-24*

He healeth the broken in heart,

and bindeth up their wounds.

Psalm 147:3

Turn you at my reproof: behold, I will pour out My spirit unto you, I will make known My words unto you.

Proverbs 1:23

He that covereth his sins shall not prosper: but whoso confesseth and forsaketh them shall have mercy.

Proverbs 28:13

For thus saith the high and lofty One that inhabiteth eternity, whose name is Holy; I dwell in the high and holy place, with him also that is of a contrite and humble spirit, to revive the spirit of the humble, and to revive the heart of the contrite ones.

Isaiah 57:15

The Spirit of the Lord God is upon me; because the Lord hath anointed me to preach good tidings unto the meek; He hath sent me to bind up the broken-hearted, to proclaim liberty to the captives, and the opening of the prison to them that are bound;

To proclaim the acceptable year of the Lord, and the day of vengeance of our God; to comfort all that mourn;

Isaiah 61:1,2

And I will restore to you the years that the locust hath eaten, the cankerworm, and the caterpiller, and the palmerworm, My great army which I sent among you.

And ye shall eat in plenty, and be satisfied, and praise the name of the Lord your God, that hath dealt wondrously with you: and My people shall never be ashamed. *Joel 2:25,26*

Blessed are they that mourn: for they shall be comforted. *Matthew 5:4*

And Peter remembered the word of Jesus, which said unto him, Before the cock crow, thou shalt deny Me thrice. And he went out, and wept bitterly.

Matthew 26:75

Wherefore be ye not unwise, but understanding what the will of the Lord is. *Ephesians 5:17*

Humble yourselves in the sight of the Lord, and He shall lift you up. *James 4:10*

If we confess our sins, He is faithful and just to forgive us our sins, and to cleanse us from all unrighteousness. *1 John 1:9*

Your Children After they Leave Home

85

When They Are Beyond Your Daily Influence

And He shall be unto thee a restorer of thy life, and a nourisher of thine old age: for thy daughter in law, which loveth thee, which is better to thee than seven sons, hath born him.

Ruth 4:15

Behold, here I am: witness against me before the Lord, and before His anointed: whose ox have I taken? or whose ass have I taken? or whom have

I defrauded? whom have I oppressed? or of whose hand have I received any bribe to blind mine eyes therewith? and I will restore it you. *1 Samuel 12:3*

He restoreth my soul: He leadeth me in the paths of righteousness for His name's sake. *Psalm 23:3*

They that hate Me without a cause are more than the hairs of Mine head: they that would destroy Me, being Mine enemies wrongfully, are mighty: then I restored that which I took not away.
Psalm 69:4

Remove from me reproach and contempt; for I have kept Thy testimonies. *Psalm 119:22*

Have mercy upon us, O Lord, have mercy upon us: for we are exceedingly filled with contempt.

Our soul is exceedingly filled with the scorning of those that are at ease, and with the contempt of the proud.
Psalm 123:3,4

And My people shall dwell in a peaceable habitation, and in sure dwellings, and in quiet resting places;
Isaiah 32:18

But thus saith the Lord, Even the captives of the mighty shall be taken away, and the prey of the terrible shall be delivered: for I will contend with him that contendeth with thee, and I will save thy children. *Isaiah 49:25*

And they that shall be of thee shall build the old waste places: thou shalt raise up the foundations of many generations; and thou shalt be called, The repairer of the breach, The restorer of paths to dwell in. *Isaiah 58:12*

Give heed to me, O Lord, and hearken to the voice of them that contend with me. *Jeremiah 18:19*

For I will restore health unto thee, and I will heal thee of thy wounds, saith the Lord; because they called thee an Outcast, saying, This is Zion, whom no man seeketh after. *Jeremiah 30:17*

And I will restore to you the years that the locust hath eaten, the cankerworm, and the caterpiller, and the palmerworm, My great army which I sent among you. *Joel 2:25*

Who shall also confirm you unto the end, that ye may be blameless in the day of our Lord Jesus Christ.

1 Corinthians 1:8

For what is it wherein ye were inferior to other churches, except it be that I myself was not burdensome to you? forgive me this wrong.

2 Corinthians 12:13

Brethren, I count not myself to have apprehended: but this one thing I do, forgetting those things which are behind, and reaching forth unto those things which are before,

Philippians 3:13

Not that I speak in respect of want: for I have learned, in whatsoever state I am, therewith to be content.

Philippians 4:11

Forbearing one another, and forgiving one another, if any man have a quarrel against any: even as Christ forgave you, so also do ye.

Colossians 3:13

And forgive us our debts, as we forgive our debtors. *Matthew 6:12*

And Paul, earnestly beholding the council, said, Men and brethren, I have lived in all good conscience before God until this day. *Acts 23:1*

Who is He that condemneth? It is Christ that died, yea rather, that is risen again, Who is even at the right hand of God, Who also maketh intercession for us. *Romans 8:34*

Hast thou faith? have it to thyself before God. Happy is he that condemneth not himself in that thing which he alloweth. *Romans 14:22*

But godliness with contentment is great gain. *1 Timothy 6:6*

For God is not unrighteous to forget your work and labour of love, which ye have shewed toward His name, in that ye have ministered to the saints, and do minister. *Hebrews 6:10*

Pray for us: for we trust we have a good conscience, in all things willing to live honestly. *Hebrews 13:18*

Confess your faults one to another, and pray one for another, that ye may be healed. The effectual fervent prayer of a righteous man availeth much.
James 5:16

If we confess our sins, He is faithful and just to forgive us our sins, and to cleanse us from all unrighteousness. *1 John 1:9*

And he that keepeth His commandments dwelleth in Him, and He in him. And hereby we know that He abideth in us, by the Spirit which He hath given us. *1 John 3:24*

86

WHEN YOU HAVE MADE MISTAKES IN RAISING THEM

And the Lord said unto him, Who hath made man's mouth? or Who maketh the dumb, or deaf, or the seeing, or the blind? have not I the Lord?

Exodus 4:11

That which I see not teach Thou me: if I have done iniquity, I will do no more. *Job 34:32*

Lead me, O Lord, in Thy righteousness because of mine enemies; make Thy way straight before my face.

Psalm 5:8

I will bless the Lord, Who hath

given me counsel: my reins also instruct me in the night seasons.

Psalm 16:7

The meek will He guide in judgment: and the meek will He teach His way. *Psalm 25:9*

For Thou art my rock and my fortress; therefore for Thy name's sake lead me, and guide me. *Psalm 31:3*

I will instruct thee and teach thee in the way which thou shalt go: I will guide thee with Mine eye. *Psalm 32:8*

It is better to trust in the Lord than to put confidence in man.

Psalm 118:8

Trust in the Lord with all thine heart; and lean not unto thine own understanding.

In all thy ways acknowledge Him, and He shall direct thy paths.

Proverbs 3:5,6

And thine ears shall hear a word behind thee, saying, This is the way, walk ye in it, when ye turn to the right hand, and when ye turn to the left.
Isaiah 30:21

And I will bring the blind by a way that they knew not; I will lead them in paths that they have not known: I will make darkness light before them, and crooked things straight. These things will I do unto them, and not forsake them. *Isaiah 42:16*

Thus saith the Lord, thy Redeemer, the Holy One of Israel; I am the Lord thy God which teacheth thee to profit, which leadeth thee by the way that thou shouldest go. *Isaiah 48:17*

No weapon that is formed against thee shall prosper; and every tongue that shall rise against thee in judgment thou shalt condemn. This is the heritage of the servants of the Lord, and their righteousness is of Me, saith the Lord. *Isaiah 54:17*

But when they shall lead you, and deliver you up, take no thought beforehand what ye shall speak, neither do ye premeditate: but whatsoever shall be given you in that hour, that speak ye: for it is not ye that speak, but the Holy Ghost. *Mark 13:11*

And the apostles said unto the Lord, Increase our faith. *Luke 17:5*

For I will give you a mouth and wisdom, which all your adversaries shall not be able to gainsay nor resist. *Luke 21:15*

Howbeit when He, the Spirit of truth, is come, He will guide you into all truth: for He shall not speak of Himself; but whatsoever He shall hear, that shall He speak: and He will shew you things to come. *John 16:13*

And Paul, earnestly beholding the council, said, Men and brethren, I have lived in all good conscience before God until this day. *Acts 23:1*

And the high priest Ananias commanded them that stood by him to smite him on the mouth.

Then said Paul unto him, God shall smite thee, thou whited wall: for sittest thou to judge me after the law, and commandest me to be smitten contrary to the law?

And they that stood by said, Revilest thou God's high priest?

Then said Paul, I wist not, brethren, that he was the high priest: for it is written, Thou shalt not speak evil of the ruler of thy people.

Acts 23:2-5

Likewise the Spirit also helpeth our infirmities: for we know not what we should pray for as we ought: but the Spirit itself maketh intercession for us with groanings which cannot be uttered.

What shall we then say to these things? If God be for us, who can be against us? *Romans 8:26,31*

Now the God of hope fill you with

all joy and peace in believing, that ye may abound in hope, through the power of the Holy Ghost. *Romans 15:13*

Let us therefore come boldly unto the throne of grace, that we may obtain mercy, and find grace to help in time of need. *Hebrews 4:16*

So that we may boldly say, The Lord is my helper, and I will not fear what man shall do unto me.

Hebrews 13:6

87

When Your Grown Children Seem Unappreciative

But the children of Belial said, How shall this man save us? And they despised him, and brought him no presents. But he held his peace.

1 Samuel 10:27

The way of the Lord is strength to the upright: but destruction shall be to the workers of iniquity. *Proverbs 10:29*

The thoughts of the righteous are right: but the counsels of the wicked are deceit.

A prudent man concealeth knowledge: but the heart of fools proclaimeth foolishness.

Proverbs 12:5,23

He that is slow to wrath is of great understanding: but he that is hasty of spirit exalteth folly. *Proverbs 14:29*

A soft answer turneth away wrath: but grievous words stir up anger.
Proverbs 15:1

He that hath knowledge spareth his words: and a man of understanding is of an excellent spirit.
Proverbs 17:27

Go not forth hastily to strive, lest thou know not what to do in the end thereof, when thy neighbour hath put thee to shame.

By long forbearing is a prince persuaded, and a soft tongue breaketh the bone. *Proverbs 25:8,15*

Seest thou a man that is hasty in his words? there is more hope of a fool than of him. *Proverbs 29:20*

To every thing there is a season, and a time to every purpose under the heaven:

A time to rend, and a time to sew; a time to keep silence, and a time to speak; *Ecclesiastes 3:1,7*

Be not rash with thy mouth, and let not thine heart be hasty to utter any thing before God: for God is in heaven, and thou upon earth: therefore let thy words be few. *Ecclesiastes 5:2*

Better is the end of a thing than the beginning thereof: and the patient in spirit is better than the proud in spirit.

Be not hasty in thy spirit to be angry: for anger resteth in the bosom of fools. *Ecclesiastes 7:8,9*

It is good that a man should both hope and quietly wait for the salvation of the Lord. *Lamentations 3:26*

In your patience possess ye your souls. *Luke 21:19*

To the weak became I as weak,

that I might gain the weak: I am made all things to all men, that I might by all means save some. *1 Corinthians 9:22*

Charity suffereth long, and is kind; charity envieth not; charity vaunteth not itself, is not puffed up,

Doth not behave itself unseemly, seeketh not her own, is not easily provoked, thinketh no evil;

1 Corinthians 13:4,5

But in all things approving ourselves as the ministers of God, in much patience, in afflictions, in necessities, in distresses,

In stripes, in imprisonments, in tumults, in labours, in watchings, in fastings;

By pureness, by knowledge, by longsuffering, by kindness, by the Holy Ghost, by love unfeigned,

2 Corinthians 6:4-6

By the word of truth, by the power of God, by the armour of righteousness on the right hand and on the left,

By honour and dishonour, by evil report and good report: as deceivers, and yet true;

As unknown, and yet well known; as dying, and, behold, we live; as chastened, and not killed;

As sorrowful, yet alway rejoicing; as poor, yet making many rich; as having nothing, and yet possessing all things. *2 Corinthians 6:7-10*

For though I would desire to glory, I shall not be a fool; for I will say the truth: but now I forbear, lest any man should think of me above that which he seeth me to be, or that he heareth of me.
2 Corinthians 12:6

And the servant of the Lord must not strive; but be gentle unto all men, apt to teach, patient, *2 Timothy 2:24*

88

WHEN YOUR GROWN CHILDREN SEEM IRRESPONSIBLE

As for God, His way is perfect; the word of the Lord is tried: He is a buckler to all them that trust in Him.

2 Samuel 22:31

O Lord my God, in Thee do I put my trust: save me from all them that persecute me, and deliver me:

Psalm 7:1

The Lord also will be a refuge for the oppressed, a refuge in times of trouble. *Psalm 9:9*

And they that know Thy name will put their trust in Thee: for Thou, Lord,

hast not forsaken them that seek Thee.
Psalm 9:10

Behold, the eye of the Lord is upon them that fear Him, upon them that hope in His mercy;

To deliver their soul from death, and to keep them alive in famine.
Psalm 33:18,19

The Lord redeemeth the soul of His servants: and none of them that trust in Him shall be desolate.
Psalm 34:22

Blessed is the man whose strength is in Thee; in whose heart are the ways of them. *Psalm 84:5*

A good man sheweth favour, and lendeth: he will guide his affairs with discretion.

He shall not be afraid of evil tidings: his heart is fixed, trusting in the Lord. *Psalm 112:5,7*

Trust in the Lord with all thine

heart; and lean not unto thine own understanding. *Proverbs 3:5*

The fear of man bringeth a snare: but whoso putteth his trust in the Lord shall be safe. *Proverbs 29:25*

Thou wilt keep him in perfect peace, whose mind is stayed on Thee: because he trusteth in Thee.
Isaiah 26:3

For thus saith the Lord God, the Holy One of Israel; In returning and rest shall ye be saved; in quietness and in confidence shall be your strength: and ye would not. *Isaiah 30:15*

Blessed is the man that trusteth in the Lord, and whose hope the Lord is.
Jeremiah 17:7

For he shall be as a tree planted by the waters, and that spreadeth out her roots by the river, and shall not see when heat cometh, but her leaf shall be green; and shall not be careful in the year of drought, neither shall cease from yielding fruit. *Jeremiah 17:8*

Jesus answered and said unto them, Verily I say unto you, If ye have faith, and doubt not, ye shall not only do this which is done to the fig tree, but also if ye shall say unto this mountain, Be thou removed, and be thou cast into the sea; it shall be done.

And all things, whatsoever ye shall ask in prayer, believing, ye shall receive. *Matthew 21:21,22*

Jesus said unto him, If thou canst believe, all things are possible to him that believeth.

And straightway the father of the child cried out, and said with tears, Lord, I believe; help Thou mine unbelief. *Mark 9:23,24*

And the apostles said unto the Lord, Increase our faith. *Luke 17:5*

Now the God of hope fill you with all joy and peace in believing, that ye may abound in hope, through the power of the Holy Ghost. *Romans 15:13*

And He said unto me, My grace is sufficient for thee: for My strength is made perfect in weakness. Most gladly therefore will I rather glory in my infirmities, that the power of Christ may rest upon me. *2 Corinthians 12:9*

But let us, who are of the day, be sober, putting on the breastplate of faith and love; and for an helmet, the hope of salvation. *1 Thessalonians 5:8*

Looking unto Jesus the author and finisher of our faith; Who for the joy that was set before Him endured the cross, despising the shame, and is set down at the right hand of the throne of God. *Hebrews 12:2*

Let your conversation be without covetousness; and be content with such things as ye have: for He hath said, I will never leave thee, nor forsake thee.
Hebrews 13:5

So that we may boldly say, The Lord is my helper, and I will not fear what man shall do unto me.

Hebrews 13:6

Casting all your care upon Him; for He careth for you.

Whom resist stedfast in the faith, knowing that the same afflictions are accomplished in your brethren that are in the world. *1 Peter 5:7,9*

SIG 12 BACK GRIPPER 4/3/03

89

WHEN THEY ARE NOT COMMITTED TO GOD

Speak ye unto all the congregation of Israel, saying, In the tenth day of this month they shall take to them every man a lamb, according to the house of their fathers, a lamb for an house:

Then Moses called for all the elders of Israel, and said unto them, Draw out and take you a lamb according to your families, and kill the passover. *Exodus 12:3,21*

And ye shall take a bunch of hyssop, and dip it in the blood that is in the bason, and strike the lintel and the two side posts with the blood that is in the bason; and none of you shall go out at the door of his house until the morning.

For the Lord will pass through to smite the Egyptians; and when He seeth the blood upon the lintel, and on the two side posts, the Lord will pass over the door, and will not suffer the destroyer to come in unto your houses to smite you. *Exodus 12:22,23*

For this child I prayed; and the Lord hath given me my petition which I asked of Him: *1 Samuel 1:27*

And he stretched himself upon the child three times, and cried unto the Lord, and said, O Lord my God, I pray Thee, let this child's soul come into him again.

And the Lord heard the voice of Elijah; and the soul of the child came into him again, and he revived.

1 Kings 17:21,22

Doth God pervert judgment? or doth the Almighty pervert justice?

If thy children have sinned against Him, and He have cast them away for their transgression;

If thou wouldest seek unto God betimes, and make thy supplication to the Almighty;

If thou wert pure and upright; surely now He would awake for thee, and make the habitation of thy righteousness prosperous.

Though thy beginning was small, yet thy latter end should greatly increase. *Job 8:3-7*

He shall judge the poor of the people, He shall save the children of the needy, and shall break in pieces the oppressor. *Psalm 72:4*

But the mercy of the Lord is from everlasting to everlasting upon them that fear Him, and His righteousness unto children's children;

To such as keep His covenant, and to those that remember His commandments to do them. *Psalm 103:17,18*

Yea, thou shalt see thy children's children, and peace upon Israel.

Psalm 128:6

Train up a child in the way he should go: and when he is old, he will not depart from it. *Proverbs 22:6*

Therefore I say unto you, What things soever ye desire, when ye pray, believe that ye receive them, and ye shall have them. *Mark 11:24*

For the promise is unto you, and to your children, and to all that are afar off, even as many as the Lord our God shall call. *Acts 2:39*

Who shall tell thee words, whereby thou and all thy house shall be saved. *Acts 11:14*

And they said, Believe on the Lord Jesus Christ, and thou shalt be saved, and thy house. *Acts 16:31*

Who against hope believed in hope, that he might become the father of many nations, according to that which was spoken, So shall thy seed be.

And being not weak in faith, he

considered not his own body now dead, when he was about an hundred years old, neither yet the deadness of Sarah's womb:

He staggered not at the promise of God through unbelief; but was strong in faith, giving glory to God;

And being fully persuaded that, what He had promised, He was able also to perform. *Romans 4:18-21*

90

WHEN YOU FEAR THE CONSEQUENCES OF THEIR LIFESTYLE

Lead me in Thy truth, and teach me: for Thou art the God of my salvation; on Thee do I wait all the day. Mine eyes are ever toward the Lord; for He shall pluck my feet out of the net. *Psalm 25:5,15*

Thy God hath commanded thy strength: strengthen, O God, that which Thou hast wrought for us.

Psalm 68:28

Order my steps in Thy word: and let not any iniquity have dominion over me. *Psalm 119:133*

Yea, if thou criest after knowledge, and liftest up thy voice for understanding;

If thou seekest her as silver, and searchest for her as for hid treasures;

Then shalt thou understand the fear of the Lord, and find the knowledge of God. *Proverbs 2:3-5*

Strive not with a man without cause, if he have done thee no harm. *Proverbs 3:30*

Only by pride cometh contention: but with the well advised is wisdom. *Proverbs 13:10*

A wrathful man stirreth up strife: but he that is slow to anger appeaseth strife. *Proverbs 15:18*

A froward man soweth strife: and a whisperer separateth chief friends. *Proverbs 16:28*

Cast out the scorner, and contention shall go out; yea, strife and reproach shall cease. *Proverbs 22:10*

But they that wait upon the Lord shall renew their strength; they shall mount up with wings as eagles; they shall run, and not be weary; and they shall walk, and not faint. *Isaiah 40:31*

Fear thou not; for I am with thee: be not dismayed; for I am thy God: I will strengthen thee; yea, I will help thee; yea, I will uphold thee with the right hand of My righteousness.

Behold, all they that were incensed against thee shall be ashamed and confounded: they shall be as nothing; and they that strive with thee shall perish.

Thou shalt seek them, and shalt not find them, even them that contended with thee: they that war against thee shall be as nothing, and as a thing of nought.

For I the Lord thy God will hold thy right hand, saying unto thee, Fear not; I will help thee. *Isaiah 41:10-13*

Blessed are the peacemakers: for they shall be called the children of God.

Matthew 5:9

Moreover if thy brother shall trespass against thee, go and tell him his fault between thee and him alone: if he shall hear thee, thou hast gained thy brother. *Matthew 18:15*

And if a kingdom be divided against itself, that kingdom cannot stand.

And if a house be divided against itself, that house cannot stand.

Mark 3:24,25

If it be possible, as much as lieth in you, live peaceably with all men.

Romans 12:18

Let us walk honestly, as in the day; not in rioting and drunkenness, not in chambering and wantonness, not in strife and envying. *Romans 13:13*

Let us therefore follow after the

things which make for peace, and things wherewith one may edify another. *Romans 14:19*

For to one is given by the Spirit the word of wisdom; to another the word of knowledge by the same Spirit;
1 Corinthians 12:8

But without faith it is impossible to please Him: for he that cometh to God must believe that He is, and that He is a rewarder of them that diligently seek Him. *Hebrews 11:6*

If any of you lack wisdom, let him ask of God, that giveth to all men liberally, and upbraideth not; and it shall be given him. *James 1:5*

But if ye have bitter envying and strife in your hearts, glory not, and lie not against the truth.

This wisdom descendeth not from above, but is earthly, sensual, devilish.

For where envying and strife is, there is confusion and every evil work.

But the wisdom that is from above is first pure, then peaceable, gentle, and easy to be intreated, full of mercy and good fruits, without partiality, and without hypocrisy.

And the fruit of righteousness is sown in peace of them that make peace.

James 3:14-18

From whence come wars and fightings among you? come they not hence, even of your lusts that war in your members?

Ye lust, and have not: ye kill, and desire to have, and cannot obtain: ye fight and war, yet ye have not, because ye ask not. *James 4:1,2*

91

WHEN THEY BLAME YOU FOR THEIR PROBLEMS

I will bless the Lord, Who hath given me counsel: my reins also instruct me in the night seasons.

I have set the Lord always before me: because He is at my right hand, I shall not be moved. *Psalm 16:7,8*

For my love they are my adversaries: but I give myself unto prayer. *Psalm 109:4*

A soft answer turneth away wrath: but grievous words stir up anger.

The tongue of the wise useth knowledge aright: but the mouth of fools poureth out foolishness.

Proverbs 15:1,2

The heart of the righteous studieth to answer: but the mouth of the wicked poureth out evil things. *Proverbs 15:28*

The wicked flee when no man pursueth: but the righteous are bold as a lion. *Proverbs 28:1*

I, even I, am he that comforteth you: who art thou, that thou shouldest be afraid of a man that shall die, and of the son of man which shall be made as grass;

And forgettest the Lord thy maker, that hath stretched forth the heavens, and laid the foundations of the earth; and hast feared continually every day because of the fury of the oppressor, as if he were ready to destroy? and where is the fury of the oppressor?

Isaiah 51:12,13

Watch ye, stand fast in the faith, quit you like men, be strong.

1 Corinthians 16:13

For the weapons of our warfare are

not carnal, but mighty through God to the pulling down of strong holds;

Casting down imaginations, and every high thing that exalteth itself against the knowledge of God, and bringing into captivity every thought to the obedience of Christ;

2 Corinthians 10:4,5

Wherefore putting away lying, speak every man truth with his neighbour: for we are members one of another.

Be ye angry, and sin not: let not the sun go down upon your wrath:

And grieve not the Holy Spirit of God, whereby ye are sealed unto the day of redemption.

Let all bitterness, and wrath, and anger, and clamour, and evil speaking, be put away from you, with all malice:

Ephesians 4:25,26,30,31

Rejoice in the Lord alway: and again I say, Rejoice.

Let your moderation be known unto all men. The Lord is at hand.

Be careful for nothing; but in every thing by prayer and supplication with thanksgiving let your requests be made known unto God.

And the peace of God, which passeth all understanding, shall keep your hearts and minds through Christ Jesus.

Finally, brethren, whatsoever things are true, whatsoever things are honest, whatsoever things are just, whatsoever things are pure, whatsoever things are lovely, whatsoever things are of good report; if there be any virtue, and if there be any praise, think on these things.

I can do all things through Christ which strengtheneth me.

Philippians 4:4-8,13

For God hath not given us the spirit of fear; but of power, and of love, and of a sound mind. *2 Timothy 1:7*

Thou therefore, my son, be strong in the grace that is in Christ Jesus.

2 Timothy 2:1

Quenched the violence of fire, escaped the edge of the sword, out of weakness were made strong, waxed valiant in fight, turned to flight the armies of the aliens. *Hebrews 11:34*

Looking diligently lest any man fail of the grace of God; lest any root of bitterness springing up trouble you, and thereby many be defiled;
Hebrews 12:15

SPECIAL WISDOM READINGS FOR FATHERS

"THE CHRISTIAN FATHER'S TEN COMMANDMENTS"

1. Thou shalt hold no other group more important than the family unit, in all thy ways being faithful to it.
2. Thou shalt teach thy sons and daughters to love, respect and obey their parents.
3. Thou shalt be a loving and considerate husband.
4. Thou shalt not speak in a manner unbecoming to a Christian gentleman.
5. Thou shalt make Sunday a day set aside for God and worship as a family.
6. Thou shalt provide for thy family – spiritually and physically.
7. Thou shalt promote and lead family worship in thy home.

8. Thou shalt be honest in all thy dealings.
9. Thou shalt respect the desires and freedoms of thy family as individuals.
10. Thou shalt be the head of thy household, while running it with love.

-Selected, "Pulpit Helps" June 1987

"JUST LIKE HIS DAD"

"Well, what are you going to be, my boy, when you have reached manhood's years; a doctor, a lawyer, or actor great, moving throngs to laughter and tears?"

But he shook his head, as he gave reply, in a serious way he said, "I don't think I'd care to be any of them; I want to be like my dad!"

He wants to be like his Dad!

You men, Did you ever think, as you pause that the boy who watches your every move is building a set of laws?

He's molding a life you're the model for, and whether it's good or bad, depends on the kind of example set.

To the boy who'd be like his dad.

Would you have him go everywhere you go?

Have him do just the things you do?

And see everything that your eyes behold, and woo all the gods you woo?

When you see the worship that shines in the eyes of your lovable little lad, could you rest content if he gets his wish, and grows to be his dad?

It's a job that none but yourself can fill;

It's a charge you must answer for;

It's a duty to show him the road to tread ere he reaches his manhood's door.

It's a debt you owe for the greatest joy.

On this old earth to be had;

This pleasure of having a boy to raise.

Who wants to be like his dad!

-Author Unknown

A FATHER'S BLESSING

Blessed is every one that feareth the Lord; that walketh in His ways.

For thou shalt eat the labour of thine hands: happy shalt thou be, and it shall be well with thee.

Thy wife shall be as a fruitful vine by the sides of thine house: thy children like olive plants round about thy table.

Behold, that thus shall the man be blessed that feareth the Lord.

The Lord shall bless thee out of Zion: and thou shalt see the good of Jerusalem all the days of thy life.

Yea, thou shalt see thy children's children, and peace upon Israel.

Psalm 128:1-6

FAMOUS QUOTES

"Man is looking for better methods; God is looking for better men, man is God's method." *-E.M. Bounds*

"The studios perusal of the Sacred volume will make better citizens, better fathers and better husbands."

-Thomas Jefferson

"When the son goes to sowing wild oats, it's time for the father to start the threshing machine.

Will the world be better because you've lived in it—or left it?

However far a man may go, he must start from his own door.

Do not try to be anything but what you are, but try to be that perfectly.

Experience is a hard teacher because she gives the test first and lesson later.

Compassion is love in action.

The fellow who brags about how smart he is, wouldn't if he were.

A friend is someone who goes around saying nice things about you behind your back."

-"Pulpit Helps," June 1987

DECISION

Will You Accept Jesus As Your Personal Savior Today?

The Bible says, "That if thou shalt confess with thy mouth the Lord Jesus, and shalt believe in thine heart that God hath raised Him from the dead, thou shalt be saved" (Romans 10:9).

Pray this prayer from your heart today! *"Dear Jesus, I believe that You died for me and rose again on the third day. I confess I am a sinner...I need Your love and forgiveness...Come into my heart. Forgive my sins. I receive Your eternal life. Confirm Your love by giving me peace, joy and supernatural love for others. Amen."*

DR. MIKE MURDOCK is in tremendous demand as one of the most dynamic speakers in America today.

More than 14,000 audiences in 38 countries have attended his Schools of Wisdom. Hundreds of invitations come to him from churches, colleges and business corporations. He is a noted author of over 130 books, including the best sellers, *"The Leadership Secrets of Jesus"* and *"Secrets of the Richest Man Who Ever Lived."* Thousands view his weekly television program, *"Wisdom Keys with Mike Murdock."* Many attend his Saturday School of Wisdom Breakfasts that he hosts in major cities of America.

Clip and Mail

❑ Yes, Mike! I made a decision to accept Christ as my personal Savior today. Please send me my free gift of your book *"31 Keys to a New Beginning"* to help me with my new life in Christ. *(B-48)*

Name____________________________ Birthdate____/____

Address____

City____________ State______ Zip____________________

Phone (____)___________________ E-Mail________________

(B-35)

Mail To:
The Wisdom Center · P.O. Box 99 · Denton, TX 76202
1-888-WISDOM-1 (1-888-947-3661)
Website: www.thewisdomcenter.tv

ABOUT *MIKE MURDOCK*

- Has embraced his Assignment to pursue...possess...and publish the Wisdom of God to help people achieve their dreams and goals.

- Began full-time evangelism at the age of 19, which has continued since 1966.

- Has traveled and spoken to more than 14,000 audiences in 38 countries, including East and West Africa, the Orient and Europe.

- Noted author of over 130 books, including best sellers, "*Wisdom For Winning*," "*Dream Seeds*" and "*The Double Diamond Principle*."

- Created the popular "*Topical Bible*" series for Businessmen, Mothers, Fathers, Teenagers, and the "*One- Minute Pocket Bible*" series and "*The Uncommon Life*" series.

- Has composed more than 5,700 songs such as "*I Am Blessed*," "*You Can Make It*," "*Holy Spirit This Is Your House*" and "*Jesus, Just The Mention Of Your Name*," recorded by many gospel artists.

- Is the Founder of The Wisdom Center, in Denton Texas.

- Has a weekly television program called "*Wisdom Keys With Mike Murdock*."

- Has appeared often on TBN, CBN, BET and other television network programs.

- Is a Founding Trustee on the Board of Charismatic Bible Ministries with Oral Roberts.

- Has had more than 3,500 accept the call into full-time ministry under his ministry.

JOIN THE Wisdom Key 3000 TODAY!

Dear Partner,

God has connected us!

I have asked the Holy Spirit for 3000 Special Partners who will plant a monthly Seed of $58.00 to help me bring the gospel around the world. (58 represents 58 kinds of blessing in the Bible.)

Will you become my monthly Faith Partner in The Wisdom Key 3000? Your monthly Seed of $58.00 is so powerful in helping heal broken lives. When you sow into the work of God, 4 Miracle Harvests are guaranteed in Scripture:

- Uncommon Protection (Mal. 3:10,11)
- Uncommon Favor (Lk. 6:38)
- Uncommon Health (Isa. 58:8)
- Financial Ideas and Wisdom (Deut. 8:18)

Your Faith Partner,

Mike Murdock

☐ *Yes Mike, I want to join The Wisdom Key 3000. Enclosed is my monthly Seed-Faith Promise of ☐ $58 ☐ Other $________. Please rush The Wisdom Key Partnership Pak to me today!*

☐CHECK ☐MONEY ORDER ☐AMEX ☐DISCOVER ☐MASTERCARD ☐VISA

Credit Card # ______________________ Exp. ___/___

Signature ______________________

Name ______________________ Birth Date ___/___/___

Address ______________________

City ______________ State ______ Zip ______

Phone ______________ E-Mail ______________

Your Seed-Faith offerings are used to support the Mike Murdock Evangelistic Association, The Wisdom Center and all its programs. The Ministry reserves the right to redirect funds as needed in order to carry out our charitable purpose.

Clip and mail completed form to:

THE WISDOM CENTER
P.O. Box 99, Denton, Texas 76202

1-888-WISDOM1
(1-888-947-3661)

Website:
WWW.THEWISDOMCENTER.TV

Your Rewards In Life Are Determined By The Problems You Solve.

- *3 Simple Ways To Increase Your Income In 90 Days*
- *4 Keys To Recognizing The Problems You Were Created To Solve*
- *12 Rewards Received When You Solve Problems For Others*
- *5 Important Keys To Remember When You Face A Problem*
- *2 Ways You Will Be Remembered*
- *12 Keys To Becoming An Uncommon Problem Solver*
- *6 Keys To Establishing Your Legacy*

The Wisdom Center
Book B-118 / $5
Wisdom Is The Principal Thing

Add 10% For S/H

THE WISDOM CENTER
P.O. Box 99, Denton, Texas 76202

1-888-WISDOM1
(1-888-947-3661)

Website:
WWW.THEWISDOMCENTER.TV

Learn From The Greatest.

- The Secret Of Handling Rejection
- How To Deal With The Mistakes Of Others
- 5 Power Keys For Effective Delegation To Others
- The Key To Developing Great Faith
- The Greatest Qualities Of Champions
- The Secret Of The Wealthy
- 4 Goal-Setting Techniques
- 10 Facts Jesus Taught About Money

In this dynamic and practical guidebook Mike Murdock points you directly to Jesus, the Ultimate Mentor. You'll take just a moment every day to reflect on His life and actions. And when you do, you'll discover all the key skills and traits that Jesus used... the powerful "leadership secrets" that build true, lasting achievement. Explore them. Study them. Put them to work in your own life and your success will be assured!

The Wisdom Center
Book B-91 / $10
Wisdom Is The Principal Thing

Add 10% For S/H

THE WISDOM CENTER
P.O. Box 99, Denton, Texas 76202

1-888-WISDOM1
(1-888-947-3661)

Website:
WWW.THEWISDOMCENTER.TV

Getting Past The Pain.

- 6 Essential Facts That Must Be Faced When Recovering From Divorce
- 4 Forces That Guarantee Career Success
- 3 Ways Crisis Can Help You
- 4 Reasons You Are Experiencing Opposition To Your Assignment
- How To Predict The 6 Seasons Of Attack On Your Life
- 4 Keys That Can Shorten Your Present Season Of Struggle
- 2 Important Facts You Must Know About Battle & Warfare
- 6 Weapons Satan Uses To Attack Marriages

Wisdom For Crisis Times will give you the answers to the struggle you are facing now, and any struggle you could ever face. Dr. Murdock presents practical steps to help you walk through your "Seasons of Fire."

- 96 Wisdom Keys from God's Word will direct you into the success that God intended for your life. This teaching will unlock the door to your personal happiness, peace of mind, fulfillment and success.

The Wisdom Center
Book B-40 / $9
Six Audio Tapes TS-40 / $30
Wisdom Is The Principal Thing

Add 10% For S/H

THE WISDOM CENTER
P.O. Box 99, Denton, Texas 76202

1-888-WISDOM1
(1-888-947-3661)

Website:
WWW.THEWISDOMCENTER.TV

Somebody's Future Will Not Begin Until You Enter.

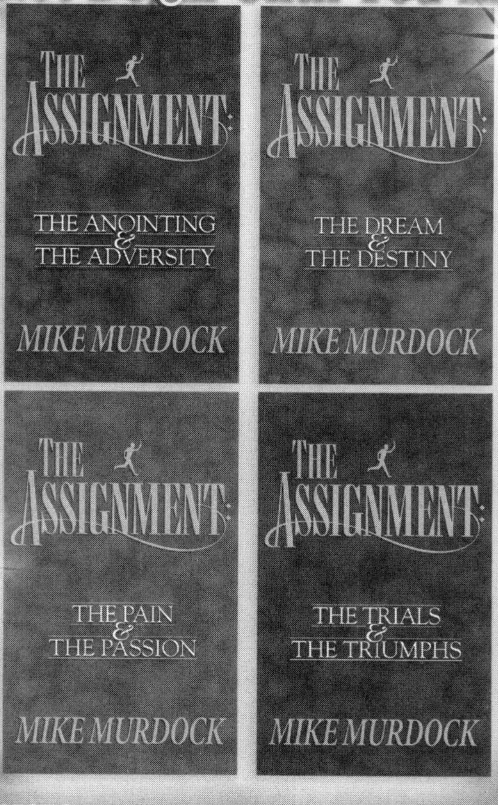

THIS COLLECTION INCLUDES 4 DIFFERENT BOOKS CONTAINING UNCOMMON WISDOM FOR DISCOVERING YOUR LIFE ASSIGNMENT

- How To Achieve A God-Given Dream And Goal
- How To Know Who Is Assigned To You
- The Purpose And Rewards Of An Enemy

The Wisdom Center
Book Pak WBL-14 / $30
Buy 3-Get 1 Free
($10 Each/$40 Value!)
Wisdom Is The Principal Thing

Add 10% For S/H

DISCOVER · MasterCard · VISA

THE WISDOM CENTER
P.O. Box 99, Denton, Texas 76202

1-888-WISDOM1
(1-888-947-3661)

Website:
WWW.THEWISDOMCENTER.TV

WISDOM 12 PAK

THE MASTER SECRET OF LIFE IS WISDOM

Ignorance Is The Only True Enemy Capable Of Destroying You (Hosea 4:6, Proverbs 11:14)

1. MY PERSONAL DREAM BOOK	B143	$5.00
2. THE COVENANT OF FIFTY-EIGHT BLESSINGS	B47	$8.00
3. WISDOM, GOD'S GOLDEN KEY TO SUCCESS	B71	$7.00
4. SEEDS OF WISDOM ON THE HOLY SPIRIT	B116	$5.00
5. SEEDS OF WISDOM ON THE SECRET PLACE	B115	$5.00
6. SEEDS OF WISDOM ON THE WORD OF GOD	B117	$5.00
7. SEEDS OF WISDOM ON YOUR ASSIGNMENT	B122	$5.00
8. SEEDS OF WISDOM ON PROBLEM SOLVING	B118	$5.00
9. 101 WISDOM KEYS	B45	$5.00
10. 31 KEYS TO A NEW BEGINNING	B48	$5.00
11. THE PROVERBS 31 WOMAN	B49	$7.00
12. 31 FACTS ABOUT WISDOM	B46	$5.00

The Wisdom Center
Book Pak WBL-12 / $30
(A $67 Value!)
Wisdom Is The Principal Thing

Add 10% For S/H

THE WISDOM CENTER
P.O. Box 99, Denton, Texas 76202

1-888-WISDOM1
(1-888-947-3661)

Website:
WWW.THEWISDOMCENTER.TV

SCHOOL of WISDOM #2

- 47 Keys In Recognizing The Mate God Has Approved For You
- 14 Facts You Should Know About Your Gifts And Talents
- 17 Important Facts You Should Remember About Your Weakness
- And Much, Much More...

- What Attracts Others Toward You
- The Secret Of Multiplying Your Financial Blessings
- What Stops The Flow Of Your Faith
- Why Some Fail And Others Succeed
- How To Discern Your Life Assignment
- How To Create Currents Of Favor With Others
- How To Defeat Loneliness

The Wisdom Center
6 Tapes | $30
PAK-002
Wisdom Is The Principal Thing

The Wisdom Center
Free Book
B-114 ($10 Value)
ENCLOSED!
Wisdom Is The Principal Thing

Add 10% For S/H

THE WISDOM CENTER
P.O. Box 99, Denton, Texas 76202
1-888-WISDOM1
(1-888-947-3661)
Website:
WWW.THEWISDOMCENTER.TV

A

UNCOMMON WISDOM FOR UNCOMMON POWER

THE Power 7

The Power 7 Pak

- Seeds of Wisdom on The Secret Place (B-115 / $5)
- Seeds of Wisdom on The Holy Spirit (B-116 / $5)
- Seeds of Wisdom on Your Assignment (B-122 / $5)
- Seeds of Wisdom on Goal Setting (B-127 / $5)
- My Personal Dream Book (B-143 / $5)
- 101 Wisdom Keys (B-45 / $5)
- 31 Keys To A New Beginning (B-48 / $5)

The Wisdom Center
All 7 Books Only $20
$35 VALUE
WBL-19
Wisdom Is The Principal Thing

Add 10% For S/H

THE WISDOM CENTER P.O. Box 99, Denton, Texas 76202
1-888-WISDOM1 (1-888-947-3661)
Website: WWW.THEWISDOMCENTER.TV

Financial Success.

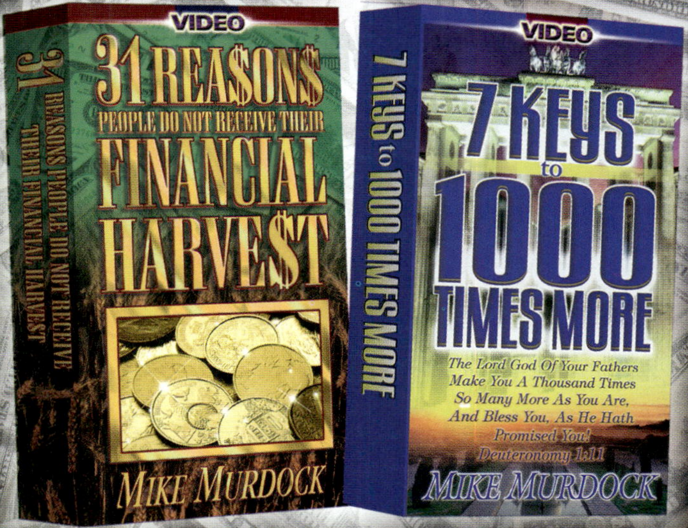

- 8 Scriptural Reasons You Should Pursue Financial Prosperity
- The Secret Prayer Key You Need When Making A Financial Request To God
- The Weapon Of Expectation And The 5 Miracles It Unlocks
- How To Discern Those Who Qualify To Receive Your Financial Assistance
- How To Predict The Miracle Moment God Will Schedule Your Financial Breakthrough
- Habits Of Uncommon Achievers
- The Greatest Success Law I Ever Discovered
- How To Discern Your Place Of Assignment, The Only Place Financial Provision Is Guaranteed
- 3 Secret Keys In Solving Problems For Others

The Wisdom Center
Video Pak AMVIDEO | $30
Buy 1-Get 1 Free
(A $60 Value!)
Wisdom Is The Principal Thing

Add 10% For S/H

THE WISDOM CENTER
P.O. Box 99, Denton, Texas 76202
1-888-WISDOM1
(1-888-947-3661)
Website:
WWW.THEWISDOMCENTER.TV

C

Songs From The Secret Place!

The Music Ministry of *MIKE MURDOCK*

The Wisdom Center
6 Tapes | $30
PAK-007
Wisdom Is The Principal Thing

The Wisdom Center
Free Book
B-100 ($10 Value)
ENCLOSED!
Wisdom Is The Principal Thing

Songs...

1. *A Holy Place*
2. *Anything You Want*
3. *Everything Comes From You*
4. *Fill This Place With Your Presence*
5. *First Thing Every Morning*
6. *Holy Spirit, I Want To Hear You*
7. *Holy Spirit, Move Again*
8. *Holy Spirit, You Are Enough*
9. *I Don't Know What I Would Do Without You*
10. *I Let Go (Of Anything That Stops Me)*
11. *I'll Just Fall On You*
12. *I Love You, Holy Spirit*
13. *I'm Building My Life Around You*
14. *I'm Giving Myself To You*
15. *I'm In Love! I'm In Love!*
16. *I Need Water (Holy Spirit, You're My Well)*
17. *In The Secret Place*
18. *In Your Presence, I'm Always Changed*
19. *In Your Presence (Miracles Are Born)*
20. *I've Got To Live In Your Presence*
21. *I Want To Hear Your Voice*
22. *I Will Do Things Your Way*
23. *Just One Day At A Time*
24. *Meet Me In The Secret Place*
25. *More Than Ever Before*
26. *Nobody Else Does What You Do*
27. *No No Walls!*
28. *Nothing Else Matters Anymore (Since I've Been In The Presence Of You Lord)*
29. *Nowhere Else*
30. *Once Again You've Answered*
31. *Only A Fool Would Try (To Live Without You)*
32. *Take Me Now*
33. *Teach Me How To Please You*
34. *There's No Place I'd Rather Be*
35. *Thy Word Is All That Matters*
36. *When I Get In Your Presence*
37. *You're The Best Thing (That's Ever Happened To Me)*
38. *You Are Wonderful*
39. *You've Done It Once*
40. *You Keep Changing Me*
41. *You Satisfy*

Add 10% For S/H

THE WISDOM CENTER
P.O. Box 99, Denton, Texas 76202
1-888-WISDOM1
(1-888-947-3661)
Website:
WWW.THEWISDOMCENTER.TV

The Uncommon Woman
Master Keys In Understanding The Man In Your Life
The One Thing Every Man Attempts To Move Away From
The Dominant Difference Between A Wrong Woman And A Right Woman
What Causes Men To Withdraw
MIKE MURDOCK
THE WISDOM FOR WOMEN SERIES
THIRTY - ONE SECRETS of an UNFORGETTABLE WOMAN
Master Secrets from the life of Ruth
THE PROVERBS 31 Woman
MIKE MURDOCK
THE WISDOM CENTER
MIKE MURDOCK•P.O. Box 99• Denton, Texas
31 Secrets of an Unforgettable Woman
The Wisdom Center
6 Tapes $30
PAK-009
Wisdom Is The Principal Thing
Free Book Enclosed!
B-49
Wisdom Is The Principal Thing
Add 10% For S/H
THE WISDOM CENTER
P.O. Box 99, Denton, Texas 76202
1-888-WISDOM1
(1-888-947-3661)
Website:
WWW.THEWISDOMCENTER.TV
E

UNCOMMON WISDOM FOR AN UNCOMMON MINISTRY

FOR *Ministers* ONLY!

Volume 1	B-107
Volume 2	B-108
Volume 3	B-109
Volume 4	B-110
Volume 5	B-111
Volume 6	B-112
Volume 7	B-113

The Wisdom Center
7 Books for Only
$20
$35 VALUE
PAKUM-1
Wisdom Is The Principal Thing

When God wants to touch a nation, He raises up a preacher. It is Uncommon Men and Women of God who have driven back the darkness and shielded the unlearned and rebellious from devastation by satanic forces. They offer the breath of life to a dead world. They open Golden Doors to Change. They unleash Forces of Truth in an age of deception.

An Uncommon Minister is prepared through seasons of pain, encounters with God, and mentors. Having sat at the feet of Uncommon Mentors his entire life, Dr. Mike Murdock shares practical but personal keys to increase the excellence and productivity of your ministry. Each volume of "The Uncommon Minister" is handy, convenient and easy to read. Your load will be lighter, your journey happier, and your effectiveness increased in "doing the will of the Father."

Add 10% For S/H

F

THE WISDOM CENTER
P.O. Box 99, Denton, Texas 76202

1-888-WISDOM1
(1-888-947-3661)

Website:
WWW.THEWISDOMCENTER.TV

What Every Parent Has Been Waiting For...

A 12-Month Family Mentorship Program.
Over 365 Chapters Of Wisdom For Every Day Of The Year.

- 31 Keys To A New Beginning
- 31 Facts About Wisdom
- 31 Secrets of an Unforgettable Woman
- The Holy Spirit Handbook
- The Assignment: Volumes 1-4
- 31 Reasons People Do Not Receive Their Financial Harvest
- Secrets of The Richest Man Who Ever Lived
- The 3 Most Important Things In Your Life
- 31 Secrets To Career Success

The Wisdom Center
Only $89
WBL-16 / $111 Value
Wisdom Is The Principal Thing

Add 10% For S/H

THE WISDOM CENTER P.O. Box 99, Denton, Texas 76202
1-888-WISDOM1 (1-888-947-3661)
Website: WWW.THEWISDOMCENTER.TV

$1,985.00
A 40% Discount!
Plus
A 72" Book Rack Display FREE!

BOOK STORE SPECIAL!

The Wisdom Center *Book Display* is available at last!

YOUR WHOLESALE PRICE

Your price for these 445 Wisdom Books (42 different titles) is only $1,985.00 ...a 40% discount. (Retail value of Books and Display Stand is $3,674.00)

FREE BOOK DISPLAY

Beautiful wood grain 72" Book Rack...holding up to 48 titles! It is a square, revolving Book Rack with clear plastic book shelves. The base is on casters for easy mobility...*only 18" of floor space!*

ORDER TODAY!

When you order today, The Wisdom Center will include this splendid 72" *Book Display* Book Rack for No Additional Cost!

WBD-72

Shipping cost of entire display and books an additional...$199.00

To place your order, contact:

H

THE WISDOM CENTER
P.O. Box 99, Denton, Texas 76202

1-888-WISDOM1
(1-888-947-3661)

Website:
WWW.THEWISDOMCENTER.TV

The Wisdom Center *Book Display* (72")

THE WISDOM CENTER BOOK DISPLAY CONTAINS 445 BOOKS!

Slot #	Item #	Title Of Books	Quantity	Retail Cost Per Book	Total Retail Value
1	B-01	Wisdom For Winning	5	$10.00 ea	$50.00
2	B-01	Wisdom For Winning	5	$10.00 ea	$50.00
3	B-11	Dream Seeds	12	$9.00 ea	$108.00
4	B-26	The God Book	7	$10.00 ea	$70.00
5	B-27	The Jesus Book	7	$10.00 ea	$70.00
6	B-28	The Blessing Bible	6	$10.00 ea	$60.00
7	B-29	The Survival Bible	6	$10.00 ea	$60.00
8	B-40	Wisdom For Crisis Times	9	$9.00 ea	$81.00
9	B-42	One-Minute Businessman's Devotional	5	$12.00 ea	$60.00
10	B-43	One-Minute Businesswoman's Devotional	5	$12.00 ea	$60.00
11	B-44	31 Secrets For Career Success	9	$10.00 ea	$90.00
12	B-45	101 Wisdom Keys	17	$5.00 ea	$85.00
13	B-46	31 Facts About Wisdom	15	$5.00 ea	$75.00
14	B-47	Covenant Of Fifty-Eight Blessings	10	$8.00 ea	$80.00
15	B-48	31 Keys To A New Beginning	15	$5.00 ea	$75.00
16	B-49	The Proverbs 31 Woman	13	$7.00 ea	$91.00
17	B-54	31 Greatest Chapters In The Bible	5	$10.00 ea	$50.00
18	B-57	31 Secrets Of An Unforgettable Woman	8	$9.00 ea	$72.00
19	B-71	Wisdom: God's Golden Key To Success	11	$7.00 ea	$77.00
20	B-72	Double Diamond Daily Devotional	3	$15.00 ea	$45.00
21	B-74	The Assignment Vol. 1: The Dream And The Destiny	8	$10.00 ea	$80.00
22	B-75	The Assignment Vol. 2: The Anointing And The Adversity	7	$10.00 ea	$70.00
23	B-82	31 Reasons People Do Not Receive Their Financial Harvest	5	$12.00 ea	$60.00
24	B-82	31 Reasons People Do Not Receive Their Financial Harvest	5	$12.00 ea	$60.00
25	B-91	The Leadership Secrets Of Jesus	6	$10.00 ea	$60.00
26	B-91	The Leadership Secrets Of Jesus	6	$10.00 ea	$60.00
27	B-92	Secrets Of Journey Vol. 1	15	$5.00 ea	$75.00
28	B-93	Secrets Of Journey Vol. 2	15	$5.00 ea	$75.00
29	B-97	The Assignment Vol. 3: The Trials And The Triumph	7	$10.00 ea	$70.00
30	B-98	The Assignment Vol. 4: The Pain And The Passion	7	$10.00 ea	$70.00
31	B-99	Secrets Of The Richest Man Who Ever Lived	6	$10.00 ea	$60.00
32	B-99	Secrets Of The Richest Man Who Ever Lived	6	$10.00 ea	$60.00
33	B-100	Holy Spirit Handbook Vol. 1	8	$10.00 ea	$80.00
34	B-101	The 3 Most Important Things In Your Life	5	$10.00 ea	$50.00
35	B-101	The 3 Most Important Things In Your Life	5	$10.00 ea	$50.00
36	B-104	7 Keys To 1000 Times More	8	$10.00 ea	$80.00
37	B-104	7 Keys To 1000 Times More	8	$10.00 ea	$80.00
38	B-107	The Uncommon Minister Vol. 1	15	$5.00 ea	$75.00
39	B-108	The Uncommon Minister Vol. 2	15	$5.00 ea	$75.00
40	B-114	The Law Of Recognition	5	$10.00 ea	$50.00
41	B-114	The Law Of Recognition	5	$10.00 ea	$50.00
42	B-115	Seeds Of Wisdom On The Secret Place Vol.13	15	$5.00 ea	$75.00
43	B-116	Seeds Of Wisdom On The Holy Spirit Vol.14	15	$5.00 ea	$75.00
44	B-117	Seeds Of Wisdom On The Word Of God Vol.15	15	$5.00 ea	$75.00
45	B-118	Seeds Of Wisdom On Problem Solving Vol.16	15	$5.00 ea	$75.00
46	B-122	Seeds Of Wisdom On Your Assignment Vol.20	15	$5.00 ea	$75.00
47	B-127	Seeds Of Wisdom On Goal-Setting Vol.25	15	$5.00 ea	$75.00
48	B-137	Seeds Of Wisdom On Productivity Vol.27	15	$5.00 ea	$75.00

Total of 445 Books and Display ~~$3,674.00~~

$1,985.00

THE WISDOM CENTER P.O. Box 99, Denton, Texas 76202

1-888-WISDOM1 (1-888-947-3661)

Website: WWW.THEWISDOMCENTER.TV

GIFTS OF WISDOM...

SPECIALTY *Bibles*

*Each Book Sold Separately

- **The Businessman s Topical Bible** (B-33 / $10)
- **The Children s Topical Bible** (B-154 / $10)
- **The Father s Topical Bible** (B-35 / $10)
- **The Grandparent s Topical Bible** (B-34 / $10)
- **The Minister s Topical Bible** (B-32 / $10)
- **The Mother s Topical Bible** (B-36 / $10)
- **The New Believer s Topical Bible** (B-37 / $10)
- **The Seeds of Wisdom Topical Bible** (B-31 / $10)
- **The ServiceMan s Topical Bible** (B-138 / $10)
- **The Teen s Topical Bible** (B-30 / $10)
- **The Traveler s Topical Bible** (B-139 / $10)
- **The Widow s Topical Bible** (B-38 / $10)

The Wisdom Center
Only $10
Wisdom Is The Principal Thing

Add 10% For S/H

THE WISDOM CENTER P.O. Box 99, Denton, Texas 76202

1-888-WISDOM1 (1-888-947-3661)

Website: WWW.THEWISDOMCENTER.TV

My Gift Of Appreciation...

The Wisdom Commentary

The Wisdom Commentary includes 52 topics...for mentoring your family every week of the year.

These topics include:

- Abilities
- Achievement
- Anointing
- Assignment
- Bitterness
- Blessing
- Career
- Change
- Children
- Dating
- Depression
- Discipline
- Divorce
- Dreams And Goals
- Enemy
- Enthusiasm
- Favor
- Finances
- Fools
- Giving
- Goal-Setting
- God
- Happiness
- Holy Spirit
- Ideas
- Intercession
- Jobs
- Loneliness
- Love
- Mentorship
- Ministers
- Miracles
- Mistakes
- Money
- Negotiation
- Prayer
- Problem-Solving
- Protégés
- Satan
- Secret Place
- Seed-Faith
- Self-Confidence
- Struggle
- Success
- Time-Management
- Understanding
- Victory
- Weaknesses
- Wisdom
- Word Of God
- Words
- Work

Gift Of Appreciation
For Your Sponsorship Seed of $100 or More
Gift Of Appreciation

My Gift Of Appreciation To My Sponsors! ...Those Who Sponsor One Square Foot In The Completion Of The Wisdom Center!

Thank you so much for becoming a part of this wonderful project...The completion of The Wisdom Center! The total purchase and renovation cost of this facility (10,000 square feet) is just over $1,000,000. This is approximately $100 per square foot. **The Wisdom Commentary is my Gift of Appreciation for your Sponsorship Seed of $100...that sponsors one square foot of The Wisdom Center. Become a Sponsor!** You will love this Volume 1, of The Wisdom Commentary. It is my exclusive Gift of Appreciation for The Wisdom Key Family who partners with me in the Work of God as a Sponsor.

Add 10% For S/H

THE WISDOM CENTER P.O. Box 99, Denton, Texas 76202

1-888-WISDOM1 (1-888-947-3661)

Website: WWW.THEWISDOMCENTER.TV

UNCOMMON WISDOM FOR UNCOMMON LEADERS

Leadership

Leadership 4

- **Wisdom For Winning** (B-01 / $10)
- **Dream Seeds** (B-11 / $9)
- **The Leadership Secrets Of Jesus** (B-91 / $10)
- **Wisdom For Crisis Times** (B-40 / $9)

The Wisdom Center
All 4 Books!
Only $30 $38 Value
WBL-4
Wisdom Is The Principal Thing

Add 10% For S/H

L

THE WISDOM CENTER
P.O. Box 99, Denton, Texas 76202

1-888-WISDOM1
(1-888-947-3661)

Website:
WWW.THEWISDOMCENTER.TV

Master Secrets To Uncommon Increase.
7 KEYS to 1000 TIMES MORE
The Lord God Of Your Fathers Make You A Thousand Times So Many More As You Are, And Bless You, As He Hath Promised You!
MURDOCK
31 REAON PEOPLE DO NOT RECEIVE THEIR FINANCIAL HARVE$T
MIKE MURDOCK
THE WISDOM CENTER
MIKE MURDOCK • P.O. Box 99 • Denton, Texas
7 KEYS to 1000 TIMES MORE
The Wisdom Center
6 Tapes | $30
PAK-008
Wisdom Is The Principal Thing
Free Book
B-82 ($12 Value)
Enclosed!
Wisdom Is The Principal Thing
The Greatest Success Law I Ever Discovered
7 Reasons God Wants To Increase Your Finances
58 Important Facts About Obedience
Add 10% For S/H
THE WISDOM CENTER
P.O. Box 99, Denton, Texas 76202
1-888-WISDOM1
(1-888-947-3661)
Website:
WWW.THEWISDOMCENTER.TV
M

The Wisdom Journal

"Write The Things Which Thou Hast Seen, And The Things Which Are, And The Things Which Shall Be Hereafter."

-Revelation 1:19

Stunningly beautiful Black and Gold Leatherette. Contains 160 pages for your personal journalizing and diary...a different Wisdom Key for each day...it also includes:

- 101 Wisdom Keys
- 31 Facts About Favor
- 31 Facts About Wisdom
- 31 Facts About The Holy Spirit
- 31 Qualities Of An Unforgettable Woman
- 58 Leadership Secrets Of Jesus
- Read The Bible Through In A Year Program
- Sample Page For Effective Note Taking

The Wisdom Center
$20 Each
B-163
Wisdom Is The Principal Thing

Add 10% For S/H

N

THE WISDOM CENTER
P.O. Box 99, Denton, Texas 76202

1-888-WISDOM1
(1-888-947-3661)

Website:
WWW.THEWISDOMCENTER.TV

JOIN THE Wisdom Key 3000 TODAY!

Dear Partner,

God has connected us!

I have asked the Holy Spirit for 3000 Special Partners who will plant a monthly Seed of $58.00 to help me bring the gospel around the world. (58 represents 58 kinds of blessing in the Bible.)

Will you become my monthly Faith Partner in The Wisdom Key 3000? Your monthly Seed of $58.00 is so powerful in helping heal broken lives. When you sow into the work of God, 4 Miracle Harvests are guaranteed in Scripture:

- Uncommon Protection (Mal. 3:10,11)
- Uncommon Favor (Lk. 6:38)
- Uncommon Health (Isa. 58:8)
- Financial Ideas and Wisdom (Deut. 8:18)

Your Faith Partner,

Mike Murdock

☐ ***Yes Mike, I want to join The Wisdom Key 3000. Enclosed is my monthly Seed-Faith Promise of ☐ $58 ☐ Other $__________. Please rush The Wisdom Key Partnership Pak to me today!***

☐CHECK ☐MONEY ORDER ☐AMEX ☐DISCOVER ☐MASTERCARD ☐VISA

Credit Card # ____________________________ Exp. ___/___

Signature ____

Name ____________________________ Birth Date ___/___/___

Address ____

City ________________________ State ______ Zip _______

Phone __________________ E-Mail ____________________

Your Seed-Faith offerings are used to support the Mike Murdock Evangelistic Association, The Wisdom Center and all its programs. The Ministry reserves the right to redirect funds as needed in order to carry out our charitable purpose.

Clip and mail completed form to:

THE WISDOM CENTER P.O. Box 99, Denton, Texas 76202

1-888-WISDOM1 (1-888-947-3661)

Website: WWW.THEWISDOMCENTER.TV

0

UNCOMMON WISDOM FOR UNCOMMON ACHIEVERS

Dream 7 PAK

- **The Leadership Secrets Of Jesus** (B-91 / $10)
- **Dream Seeds** (B-11 / $9)
- **Secrets Of The Richest Man Who Ever Lived** (B-99 / $10)
- **The Assignment; The Dream And The Destiny, Volume 1** (B-74 / $10)
- **The Holy Spirit Handbook** (B-100 / $10)
- **The Law Of Recognition** (B-114 / $10)
- **31 Reasons People Do Not Receive Their Financial Harvest** (B-82 / $12)

The Wisdom Center
7 Books for only $50 $71 Value
WBL-23
Wisdom Is The Principal Thing

Add 10% For S/H

P

THE WISDOM CENTER
P.O. Box 99, Denton, Texas 76202

1-888-WISDOM1
(1-888-947-3661)

Website:
WWW.THEWISDOMCENTER.TV